Walking Straight in a Crooked World

Walking Straight
in a
Crooked World

Don M. Aycock

BROADMAN PRESS
Nashville, Tennessee

© Copyright 1987 • Broadman Press
All Rights Reserved
4250-34
ISBN: 0-8054-5034-3
Dewey Decimal Classification: 248.4
Subject Headings: CHRISTIAN LIFE // DISCIPLESHIP
Library of Congress Catalog Number: 86-17193
Printed in the United States of America

Unless otherwise stated, all Scripture quotations are from the HOLY
BIBLE: *New International Version,* copyright © 1978, New York Bible
Society. Used by permission.
Scripture quotations marked RSV are from the Revised Standard Version
of the Bible, copyrighted 1946, 1952, © 1971, 1973.
Scripture quotations marked GNB are from the *Good News Bible,* the
Bible in Today's English Version. Old Testament: Copyright © American
Bible Society 1976; New Testament: Copyright © American Bible Society
1966, 1971, 1976. Used by permission.

Library of Congress Cataloging-in-Publication Data

Aycock, Don M.
  Walking straight in a crooked world.

  1. Fruit of the Spirit.   2. Spiritual life—Baptist
authors.   I. Title.
BV4501.2.A96   1987   234'.13   86-17193
ISBN 0-8054-5034-3

*I dedicate this book, which is about life,
to the people who gave me life—my parents,
Dewey and Mabel Aycock*

Preface

When I was ten years old we attended a fair in a town near our home. The variety of stomach-murdering food was a pure joy to a little boy who loved junk food. The booths with balloons for bursting and the stalls with BB guns (for shooting out a star on a piece of cardboard) were lures to induce boys into spending their hard-earned quarters.

But the most memorable attraction was the fun house. The fun house had walls of glass, so I was not sure if I could go straight, and mirrors in one room that made me look at least seven feet tall. What I remember most, though, was the entrance. To enter the fun house you had to walk across a bridge-like structure that swayed up and down and back and forth.

In the years since my first trip to that fun house, I have often thought of the moving floor at the entrance. It seems like a parable about life. We seemingly try to do the best we can, yet it appears as if the very foundations buckle under our feet and sway, throwing us off balance. We might do well were it not for the moving paths we travel. Our world reminds me of that spaghetti Western, "The Good, the Bad, and the Ugly." We receive mixed images. At times, the world itself is crooked. This presents a dilemma for believers: How can one *walk straight in a crooked world?*

The apostle Paul wrote his letter to the Galatians, hoping to help them learn what freedom in Christ is, and to appropriate that freedom as the moving force in their lives. In 5:22-25 Paul listed "the fruit of the Spirit" and urged his readers to live by the Spirit. He wrote: "But the fruit of the Spirit is love, joy, peace, patience, kindness, goodness, faithfulness, gentleness and self-control. Against such things there is no law. Those who belong to Christ Jesus have crucified the sinful nature, its passions and desires. Since we live by the Spirit, let us keep in step with the Spirit."

These fruit of the Spirit are precisely the steadying and energizing forces which can help us walk straight in a crooked world. They have to do with our inner lives of faith and devotion, with our relationships toward others around us, and with our love for the Heavenly Father. As such, these matters represent some of the most basic Christian ethics, values, and virtues. Paul did not use the plural—"fruits"— here, but instead employed the singular—"fruit." I think this is because he was not referring to many paths of the Spirit but to a wholistic view of spiritual life. A sound spiritual life will contain, not some of these elements, but all of them to some degree. It is like a hub with many spokes or a tree with many branches. The goal is to seek the fruit of the Spirit as a unified whole instead of a fragmented and piecemeal vision.

Those who live out of the power and values of the fruit of the Spirit can cope all right, but more than that. After all, in Christ we are "more than conquerors through him who loved us" (Rom. 8:37). These basic aspects of faith help us to deal with whatever comes our way and transform it all for our betterment and the glory of God. Author John Baillie expressed this hope in one of his prayers:

Teach me, O God, so to use all the circumstances of my life today that they may bring forth in me the fruits of holiness rather than the fruits of sin.

Let me use disappointment as material for patience:
Let me use success as material for thankfulness:
Let me use suspense as material for perseverance:
Let me use danger as material for courage:
Let me use reproach as material for long suffering:
Let me use praise as material for humility:
Let me use pleasures as material for temperance:
Let me use pains as material for endurance.[1]

An old proverb goes, "Eagles don't flock. You have to find them one at a time." In one sense this is true of Christian values. Finding them one at a time is what this book is all about. I have devoted one chapter to each of the elements which Paul mentions in Galatians 5:22, and have added an "Epilogue" on walking in the Spirit. If you are helped through these efforts to walk straight in a crooked world, then my goal will have been satisfied.

The members of the Enon Baptist Church in Franklinton, Louisiana, have heard these ideas in a different form. They help keep me straight! My major professor in my doctoral studies, Dr. Fisher Humphreys, has helped me understand more of the depth, width, length, and beauty of the Christian faith. I will always be grateful to him for his strength of thought and gentleness of spirit. My wife, Carla, and our twin boys, Ryan and Chris, keep life hopping for Pop and make living with them fun. Much of what I know about joy I learned from them.

DON M. AYCOCK

Contents

1
It Makes the World
Go 'Round—Love

When God measures a man, He puts the tape around his
heart—not his head.—Guideposts

My '65 pickup lunged forward as I headed home for the weekend.
I was beginning my second year of college, and it was becoming more
difficult. I had come from a rural community and arrived on a campus
with thousands of students. The Sixties atmosphere of rebellion and
general suspicion of everyone over thirty hung like a shroud over the
campus. A shy kid from the "sticks" had a tough time ever feeling
at home in a place like that. But others had done it, and I could see
no reason why I could not make it, too.

Then the "crisis" hit me like a hurricane. The crisis was a question
which haunted me: "Who am I, and does anyone care if I live or die?"
Many of my friends were going to Vietnam. Some were not returning.
Others were heavily into drugs, and from their behavior they might
as well have been in Southeast Asia.

I was fortunate. The draft had not summoned me, and drugs had
never interested me in the least. I attended a local church and even
taught a youth Sunday School class. But all of that could not quieten
my mind which seemed like a dog growling in the basement. That
hurting question kept surfacing, and nothing could appease its raven-
ous appetite for long. I dished out hors d'oeuvres of logic. *You know*
who you are. You are Dewey and Mabel Aycock's son. You were born
in Texas and lived most of your life in Evangeline, Louisiana. You
worked on a rice farm and as a roughneck in the oilfields to go to school.
You love music and the things of God. Still, the dog in the basement
kept growling its question: "Yes, but who are *you*, and does anyone
really care?"

I also tossed out scraps of desperation. *Don't you know that every-*

body *is feeling like this? Don't you realize that* nobody *feels perfectly ok?* But these scraps did not last long and were soon digested by that beast in the basement who never let up in its quest for an answer to . . . *Who are you, and does anyone care?*

A lady in my church was wise in the ways of God and of men, and she saw right through me. At the time I could not realize exactly how, although I now understand she was gifted in working with teenagers and could empathize with them. This lady often invited a bunch of us students to her home where we could enjoy a good meal with her husband and children. I began to realize she was extra special—not simply a mother figure, but a genuine friend who cared how I felt and what I thought.

She used to ask about my family and often conducted me on trips of memory. On those occasions of remembering I finally came to answer the question which had tortured me so long.

As I drove home that fall weekend, it was for a reunion with a part of me which had been left behind. How my truck stayed on the road I do not know. I cried all the way home at the incredible realization of the answer to my question: "Who am I?" The answer came: *I am my parents' son. I am growing and maturing and realizing the answer to the second question—"Does anyone care?"* The answer was an undeniable, unswerving *Yes! Someone* does *care. I am loved.* I was not going crazy that afternoon. I was *going sane.*

This answer had always been part of me, but there are times when a person needs to *feel* loved. At times the distance between the head and the heart is more than a matter of eighteen inches. It is sometimes measured by the yardstick of longtime struggle, pain, and doubt, and by the ruler of regret.

Driving home that afternoon gave me a chance to reflect on my life. Various images displayed themselves on the screen of my memory. I was no casual observer but was the cast, the director, and the stage hand! I saw a boy of seven or eight come into the living room with his BB gun slung over his shoulder. As he passed by the old black-and-white TV, the BB gun went off and shot out the picture tube. Panic and fear seized the boy, and he was sure his parents would, too. Instead, a loving mother and father decided that their little boy was worth far more than an old TV set. They assured him it was not his fault, and that the BB had not even come close to the TV. It merely "happened" to explode about the same time as the boy walked in front of it. To a terrified kid such an explanation seems perfectly logical, and it was happily accepted as the true account of the TV's demise. Only later did he figure out what actually happened and why his parents "stretched" the facts a bit. I was loved.

The second feature came on. It showed that same boy, now about ten or twelve. He was in a Texas oilfield where his father was a toolpusher (the foreman on a drilling rig). A truck from a chemical supply company came lumbering down the board road toward the drilling site. The driver turned around and began backing up to the supply house. He backed his truck into the radiator of a large diesel engine used to pump the drilling fluids.

The truck driver stopped when he felt the bump and jumped out to see what had happened. He saw the boy standing there watching the accident. The toolpusher came running over. Before he could speak a word the truck driver falsified, "That kid over there was in my way. I didn't want to run over him so I had to swing around him. That's why I hit the pump. It's his fault." The boy was stunned, but within seconds he saw his father stand face to face with the driver.

He yelled over the roar of the rig noise, "I saw exactly what happened. The boy was standing over here way out of your way. He didn't have anything to do with it. You're just a bad driver who tore up my radiator. It's *your* fault, and your company is going to pay for getting it fixed. Got it?" The driver weakly nodded, pulled his truck out of the pierced radiator, and unloaded his supplies. Later the toolpusher carried the radiator to have it fixed, and the boy went along. I will never forget the toolpusher's words: "I know that wasn't your fault so don't worry about it. And if anyone ever tries to blame you for something like that again, you come tell me. We'll get it straight in a hurry."

Parents sometimes overprotect their children and never let them live up to the consequences of their own actions. Others always assume the worst about their kids, blaming everything on them, even if it was not their fault. My parents knew the difference, and that day in a Texas oilfield many years ago is riveted to my memory. I was loved.

I also saw a father standing behind his son, with his arms draped over the boy's shoulders and making a "V" across the boy's chest. He proudly told his associates at work, "This is my son." I saw parents presenting their eighth-grade son a brand-new Bundy trumpet, because he wanted to be a musician. New trumpets cost hard-earned money, but they cared about what their son cared about.

I watched the rerun of a father giving his boy a guitar and asking in later years, "Hey, get your guitar and play us a tune." I saw the boy, his brother, and their father make a wooden boat to fish Bayou Des Canes, and spent many joyful hours hauling in bluecats off a trot line. I saw the boy in a garden working side by side with his father. The boy hated planting a garden, but he liked working with the older man.

The replaying of those memories, along with many others, had a healing effect on me as I struggled to answer the perennial teenage question.

There are memories of a totally different kind, too. I recall the times when too much alcohol flowed around our house when I was growing up (none does now). I remember an older brother who was always a mystery to me, a brother with whom I never did communicate well. I look back on times when my father worked away from home, and I longed to talk with him. But these negative scenes have little power to affect me now, because the vignettes in which I felt loved, appreciated, and accepted now dominate my mental and emotional landscape. Truly, love is a healer of human hurts.

Love and God

When Paul referred to the fruit of the Spirit as love, I feel sure he had many ideas in mind. He primarily meant that astounding love God has for His children.

I feel tongue-tied here. To speak about the love of God is like speaking of the universe. I cannot even imagine it, so I will have to do what scientists do with the universe—break it down into smaller parts. They speak of galaxies such as the Milky Way, of individual planets such as the Earth, of specific countries like the United States, of particular states like Louisiana, of definite places like New Orleans; of specific individuals such as I.

First John 4:7-21 is one of the most amazing passages in the entire Bible. It begins and ends with the affirmation that love is from God from first to last. "God is love." This is a far cry from the "Unmoved Mover" or "that than which nothing greater can be conceived" of the philosophers. Because God is love, I am. I exist through the goodness of His letting there be life. He spoke the word, "Let there be light," and there was light. In a similar manner, God stated, "Let there be Don," and there was Don! God expresses His love through His letting be. He lets people, plants, and an entire universe be. This letting be calls persons into existence and leads them on, hopefully to reach the full potential of their lives. God confers himself in the lives of those who welcome him. He sustains life and works on its creative possibilities. We are because God lets us be, and He lets us be because He is love.

This gives us a clue to the meaning of life and of the Christian faith. The God Who created all things and lower creatures found little pleasure in them until He created mankind who, like God Himself, can love and be loved. Thus, it is while I love and allow myself to be loved that I am most like God. Piety does not mean I "play God." It does mean that I allow myself to live in the relationship for which God most completely fit me, namely, love.

Francis de Sales (1567-1622) wrote a devotional guide entitled *Introduction to the Devout Life*. In this guide he reflected on the love of God and the need of people to love Him. He felt that God wants the love of people as expressed through their devotion to him. De Sales wrote:

> True devotion . . . presupposes not a partial but a thorough love of God. For inasmuch as divine love adorns the soul, it is called grace, making us pleasing to the Divine Majesty; inasmuch as it gives us the strength to do good, it is called charity; but when it has arrived at that degree of perfection by which it not only makes us do well but also work diligently, frequently, and readily, then it is called devotion.[1]

God's love can be conceived in an abstract, detached manner, but de Sales was on target in thinking about it in personal and intimate terms.

I wrote at the beginning of this chapter of the crisis which changed my life. God, in His love, uses every sort of crisis through which to communicate his care. That is the meaning of Easter Sunday. That is what any crisis of separation is, whether death, a child leaving home, a divorce, whatever. During those times, when we must look our solitude squarely in the face, we discover that the face is friendly. God is there because God is love.

First John 4:18 asserts, "There is no fear in love. But perfect love drives out fear." God frees me to love myself, knowing full well that I am far from perfect—but still OK if I am in Him. He frees me to love my family, even though my love is not fully mature and they do not fully respond to me. God frees me to love my friends, even though they sometimes disappoint me and I may let them down. The Lord Jesus Christ, the God-man, comes to me with an offer of eternal love. I can refuse only at my own peril. "But perfect love drives out fear." So I am open to God's love as I am open to a friend or my beloved wife and children. It is here that I find myself "at home" in His presence, accepted as His child, protected as His precious creation.

Love and Marriage

Growth and healing come not only of parental and divine love, but of married love as well. Many a person who has felt unloved in youth has learned to be loved, and to *feel* it, later when he loses himself in the life of another. How insightful Jesus was: "For whoever would save his life will lose it" (Matt. 16:25). He meant for me to enter so deeply into the life of another that I would no longer be the center of my universe. This happens spiritually in Christ; it also happens emotionally in marriage.

Many detractors are heralding the death of marriage, but such proclamation is extremely exaggerated. Men and women will always learn to care for each other. The survival of humanity depends on it, although procreation is by no means the only reason for marriage.

My discovery of the wonder of losing myself in the life of another person came, like many of life's gifts, unexpectedly. After my "crisis,"

I took off a semester from college and worked in a Christian coffee house across the street from the university. I had made a commitment to the Lord and had felt a definite call to ministry.

One of the options was to attend a Christian college. It was Louisiana College, a Baptist school at Pineville. My first year there I made many discoveries about truth and myself. I actually had a mind and could use it. After all, Jesus taught that we were to love God with all our mind. I regretted the close of the college year. Never before had a place and a group of people become so much a part of me, But I had no money for summer school so I had to find a job.

My brother and his wife invited me to stay with them in Freeport, Texas. He felt sure I could locate work at the chemical plant where he was employed. The day I arrived, the plant was closed by a strike!

I began scrounging around for any job. All I found was a job selling vacuum cleaners door to door. What a predicament for a budding young theologian! And I felt alone, more alone than ever before.

One day a new fellow—a super salesman—showed up at the office. He and I did not hit it off so I avoided him when I could. Yet this very man I disliked became a pivotal person in my life. One day after work he invited me to our employer's house where he and his family were staying temporarily. When I showed up a beautiful young woman answered the door. I am always suspicious of people who claim "love at first sight," but I was enraptured with her. It was not love, but it surely was something. I learned that this girl was the daughter of the super salesman! Had her father just "happened" to invite me over because he liked me or could it be . . . ?

This girl, Carla, became my friend and my confidant. We began spending every spare minute together. Although both of us resisted it, we felt drawn closer and closer together. After all, we had come together almost by accident(?), were students at schools hundreds of miles apart, and hardly had the price of a hamburger between us. My summer of isolation in Texas drew to a close, and I had mixed feelings about it. What about Carla?

Two people coming to love each other is mystery. Logic has its place, but loving is not basically logical. My keeping an interest in a girl whose father I once had disliked, and who lived hundreds of miles away was anything but logical. But Augustine put it so well: "The heart has its reasons that reason knows not of."

We went our separate ways that fall but ran up large phone and postage bills. Towards the end of that semester we both knew it was time to make a serious decision—end the relationship or commit ourselves to each other regarding the future. We decided that Carla would transfer from her university to join me at my college. We married our last semester at Louisiana College and "lived on love." We had to because we had no money. Between us we made enough to pay our thirty-five-dollars-a-week rent on two rooms, to eat a frozen dinner (that we bought three for a dollar) each evening, and to pay for books and supplies at school. Our loans and scholarships paid tuition. Most of all, though, we had each other. What else mattered? We knew that whatever came, our commitment to each other would pull us through, and it has.

Carla and I have celebrated a dozen years of married life; we are the parents of twin boys—Ryan and Christopher—who are now five years old. How can I refer to that as planned, logical, or ordinary? Yet, in its own way this is exactly what it is. Our story is unique in its details, but many, many people have had similar experiences of coming to love. People who even disliked each other at first, later end up "hitched."

I have experienced healing and nearly indescribable support in my marriage. God did not make a mistake when he set lonely people in families. Psalm 68:6a expresses it: "God sets the lonely in families." When Adam first saw Eve he exclaimed, "At last!" (Gen. 2:24).

Love, as Paul put it in Galatians 5:22, is a fruit of the Spirit. This does not mean it is an abstract, bloodless, lifeless principle. The love between a man and woman in marriage is as much the work of God as is His love for mankind. Both are theologically oriented. I think a church is the proper place for weddings, if at all possible. The building and the surroundings make a symbolic statement, "There is a Third Party involved in this union. He is the same One who said, 'Let there be light,' and also 'Let there be love.' " And behold, there are both!

Love and Friendship

I cannot consider love without thinking of friendship. These two concepts are closely related, but when was the last time you read about friendship? You can find mountains of books on love, but the pickings for friendship are pretty slim. This seems strange considering the importance of our friends. Do we merely take friendship for granted or feel it is a necessary evil? Francis Bacon wrote of friendship, "It redoubleth joys, and cutteth griefs in halves."

When I was growing up I had many friends, but only one special friend, Milton. He and I were almost inseparable. We lived a half mile apart in a rural area of South Louisiana. Together Milton and I hunted, fished, attended school, played basketball and softball, and threw cow "muffins" at each other. We swung from vines out over Bayou Des Canes, giving our Tarzan yells as we let go of the vines and hit the water. We climbed small pines, grabbing the tops of those trees and jumping out so the trees would bend, and we would get an "elevator" ride down. Sometimes the tops would snap off and our ride down would be faster than we wanted!

Milton and I would pick mayhaws in the swamps and ride around in homemade boats during flood times. He had a huge abandoned sawdust pile behind his house, and we spent many hours tunneling through the sawdust with old stockings over our heads to keep the sawdust out of our eyes and noses. We were friends indeed.

Milton and I seldom see each other now. We have gone in different directions as adults do, although I still hold him in high esteem. I learned invaluable lessons from our friendship.

Friends have time for each other. This sounds like an obvious truism, but think about it for a minute. If you are "average" (whatever that means), you probably would like to have more friends, especially those who are willing to spend time with you. I am thinking of a close friend who enjoys the same kinds of things you do—spending the afternoon in front of the TV watching a football game, going shopping (my wife's favorite hobby), or traveling to an unusual destination for a day's enjoyment. I have a friend named Bill who was in seminary with me. He and I shared a common interest—goose hunting. We spent many hours together nearly freezing to death in a goose blind on the Ballard County Wildlife Refuge in Kentucky. I am not sure about Bill, but I went hunting not so much for the meat as for the fun and diversion. We would spin every yarn we knew and laugh more than I can tell. Somehow stories seem funnier when you are in a pit below ground in 12° temperature with sleet and snow falling. To this day I have no idea how we ever bagged any geese. I have not gone in a while, and I miss those times of hilarity in a goose pit.

Friends make time for each other, not only for fun, but also for the tragic periods. I will never forget when a close friend showed up at my office. He looked haggard. When I asked what was up he explained his wife was in the hospital because of a suicide attempt. Nothing could have torn me away from him that afternoon. I have been in his shoes, too, at times when I really needed to talk with a friend. I am grateful for people who make time for me, and I try to do this in my work. Pastoral care is intensified friendship carried on by a person willing to listen—really listen—and then offer insights and support.

Friendship comes through people being open with each other, because without openness, close relations cannot develop. If I go about my life as if I were somehow totally self-sufficient, and therefore closed off to others, then I would have no friends. When I display an attitude of openness in my life, from words to deeds, I then invite others to know me. Friendship wears a "welcome" mat on its face. The strange thing about it is that if a person intentionally tries to make friends, he sometimes succeeds in driving people away instead of bringing them close. We cannot *make* someone like us. We can only be available to allow a friendship to develop. Orlo Strunk, Jr., is a counselor who sees many people in his practice. He is aware that sometimes people who come to see him treat him as if he were not a flesh-and-blood human being like them. He put it this way once:

> Your eyes have put me in a file.
> You have alphabetized me like a punched card;
>
> ....
>
> How strange that you should make a white page
> from a gray suit and a red tie!

Look closer. Don't you see the life around my eyes?
Don't you see the silent throbbing of the blue vein
    just below my index finger?
No, you don't see. You are wide-eyed and blind,
    and you think you need a punched card
    filed away.[2]

I well understand Strunk. Because I am a pastor, people often want to file me or pigeonhole me and assume that they know exactly who I am. I cannot stop people from doing so, but when they do, we both lose, because they will never come to know the real me, the me beneath the coat and tie. I know myself to be a person who, as the late Harry Chapin once put it, "when you look in his eyes you know there is somebody in there." For the person who will take the time to know me, he or she will find an honest-to-goodness human being who understands what it is to hurt and despair, as well as to exult and celebrate. To those willing to listen, I will tell about my life. To those willing to hear, I will share a sample of my Chet Atkins record collection. With those willing to be with me, I will go fishing. To those interested in seeing, I will give a demonstration of my word processor-computer. I will go about my pastoral work being kept at arm's distance by some but invited in closer by others. Only with the latter will I ever make any difference. We pastors are not God, and we do not want to be treated as such. We want to be included as real people.

Friendship is the spice of life. It thrives on novelty and good humor. A retired friend recently celebrated his birthday. For six months prior to it he had reminded our church about it: "Hey, ya'll don't forget my birthday. You've got only six months." When the much-heralded day arrived I sent him, in fun, not a traditional birthday card, but one which read on the front: "Deepest Sympathy." In church we unrolled a five-by-fifteen-foot "card" wishing him a happy birthday. He brought my card to church and showed it off. Had this man been closed to others, and had he taken himself too seriously, such would have been futile.

Friendship gives itself away. Every true friend I have is willing to give himself or herself to me in trust and mutual protection. I was the pastor of a church in Kentucky several years ago. We had several seminary students working with us in various capacities. As we prepared to leave that church, two of the students, Reid and Jean, gave us a copy of *The Velveteen Rabbit*. They marked a place in the book which was a conversation between the Skin Horse and the Rabbit. The conversation goes like this:

> "What is REAL?" asked the Rabbit one day. . . . "Does it mean having things that buzz inside you and a stick-out handle?" "Real isn't how you are made," said the Skin Horse. "It's a thing that happens to you. When a child loves you for a long, long time, not just to play with, but REALLY loves you, then you become Real." "Does it hurt?" asked the Rabbit. "Sometimes," said the Skin Horse, for he was always truthful. "When you are Real you don't mind being hurt." "Does it happen all at once, like being wound up," he asked, "or bit by bit?" "It doesn't happen all at once," said the Skin Horse. "You become. It takes a long time. That's why it doesn't often happen to people who break easily, or have sharp edges, or who have to be carefully kept. Generally, by the time you are Real, most of your hair has been loved off, and your eyes drop out and you get loose in the joints and very shabby. But these things don't matter at all, because once you are Real you can't be ugly, except to people who don't understand."[3]

Jean and Reid wrote as their inscription, "To the Aycock Family— A Real family which possesses the gift for helping others to feel Real." I treasure those words and have often gone back to that passage in the book. I have taken it as sort of a model for what I want to be to others in my friendship. I cannot be this to everyone because not everyone wants it. But to those who do, I am willing to offer it. Only love can make for good friendship.

Love: It not only makes the world go 'round. It also makes the trip worthwhile.

2
Joy to the World

Joy is the echo of God's life within us.—Joseph Marmion

Long before "Joy to the World" was a Christmas hymn, it was the insignia of the Christian church. Joy was the mark of those faithful men and women of antiquity who faced persecution with the stamina to overcome and problems with the strength to conquer. Paul called his friends to a life of joyful living which, as the fruit of the Spirit, enabled them to withstand the forces of hell itself. Consider this counsel: "Be joyful always; pray continually; give thanks in all circumstances, for this is God's will for you in Christ Jesus" (1 Thess. 5:16-17). The list is headed by joy. There is a lesson here.

The New Testament has eleven basic words associated with varieties of joy. These include exultant joy; optimism and enthusiasm; gladness; pleasure; courage; hilarity; boasting; blessedness; leaping for joy; inward joy; and shared joy.[1] The last three are most important for our purposes here.

Leaping Joy

Sometimes life is filled with the glory of God, and we behold grace in each face. Joy comes bubbling to the surface, and we feel like jumping for joy. This was not invented by kids on Christmas morning. As far back as we can remember in our faith, people have expressed their joy through movement. David danced before the Lord, even if his wife did think he had lost his mind (See 2 Sam. 6.) Luke tells us that such joy is a light, skipping movement. When Mary visited Elizabeth before the birth of either of their children, Elizabeth exulted, "As soon as the sound of your greeting reached my ears, the baby in my womb *leaped for joy*" (Luke 1:44, italics added). In Bunyan's

Pilgrim's Progress, Christian experienced forgiveness at the cross, and then "Christian gave three leaps for joy, and went on singing."

Robert Burns wrote a poem in which he expressed his feeling that an ale house was a warmer, more inviting place than a church. I know nothing about ale houses, but I do know something about churches. And as much as I hate to admit it, Burns was right in pointing out that a church can be a cold, ominous place. But it should be the focus of life and warmth, of laughter and mirth, of deep feelings expressed in significant actions. Most of all, the church should be a place of joy where people worship God with a sense of anticipation and quiet enthusiasm. How unbiblical is a drab, yawning, lethargic group of people who have dragged themselves out of bed and to the service, and who think about all else except the fact that they have more right to a leaping joy than anyone else on earth!

As I reflect on the people I have known, I remember a few who have reflected such joy. There is the woman who simply smiles at church. This seems so trivial, but as I scan the faces turned toward me on Sundays, I realize that her joy-reflecting smile is anything but trivial. There was a man, now with his Lord, for whom life was a celebration instead of a wake. He could not help but live as if life were a kind of perpetual circus, because for him it was. God did not make some sort of ghastly mistake when he gave us the gift of life, or renewed life in Christ. We can leap for joy—the sheer joy of knowing Christ and being known by him.

Inner Joy

Another sort of joy is described in the New Testament. It is an inward kind. The word "rejoice" comes from this origin. Paul used it as an imperative: "Rejoice with those who rejoice" (Rom. 12:15). Also, he promised this joy to those who are filled with the Spirit: "May the God of hope fill you with all joy and peace as you trust in him, so that you may overflow with hope by the power of the Holy Spirit" (Rom. 15:13).

Jesus spoke of this inner joy as reflecting the feeling one has over the lost coming home. "I tell you, there is rejoicing in the presence of the angels of God over one sinner who repents" (Lk. 15:10). The father in the parable of the lost son says to the older brother, "But we had to celebrate and be glad, because this brother of yours was dead and is alive again; he was lost and is found" (Luke 15:32).

In a strange and almost inexplicable way, inner joy is sometimes related to suffering. To claim that joy and suffering go together seems like saying matches and dynamite go together. But this is precisely what the New Testament affirms. Peter admonished, "But rejoice that you participate in the sufferings of Christ, so that you may be overjoyed when his glory is revealed" (1 Pet. 4:13). To participate in the full life of Christ is to take part in His sufferings as well as His glory. To have the latter without the former would give life a tilted, truncated list.

Aesop told the fable of two men walking in the woods. One found a hatchet under some brush and said, "Look what *I've* found." His companion said, "Don't say, 'Look what *I've* found.' Say, 'Look what *we've* found.' " A short while later they came upon a group of men, one of whom claimed that the hatchet was his. The man with the tool said to his friend, "It looks like we're in trouble." The friend responded, "Don't say, 'It looks like *we're* in trouble.' Say, 'It looks like *I'm* in trouble.' " Aesop knew that sharing joy and danger went together.

The Book of Hebrews has this as a major theme. The writer addressed people who had recently come to faith in Christ. "You sympathized with those in prison and joyfully accepted the confiscation of your property, because you knew that you yourselves had better and lasting possessions" (Heb. 10:34). This same writer urged followers of Christ, "Let us fix our eyes on Jesus, the author and perfecter of our faith, who for the joy set before him endured the cross, scorning its shame, and sat down at the right hand of the throne of God" (Heb. 12:2). Again, this writer referred to those with authority in the church and told Christians, "Obey them so that their work will be a joy, not a burden, for that would be of no advantage" (Heb. 13:17). To live a life of joy does not mean that trouble and pain will never come. It means that joy is a form of energy which helps people live above the circumstances of trouble.

One of the founders of Methodism was John Wesley. On March 29, 1737, he recorded these words in his Journal:

> I am convinced as true religion or holiness cannot be without cheerfulness, so steady cheerfulness, on the other hand, cannot be without holiness or true religion. And I am equally convinced that true religion has nothing sour, austere, unsociable, unfriendly in it; but, on the contrary, implies the most winning sweetness, the most amiable softness and gentleness.[2]

Wesley lived in the rough-and-tumble world of the circuit rider, but he knew that joy is not dependent on perfect circumstances. Joy is deep and causes a person to live out a joyful existence. As the Bible puts it, "A cheerful heart is good medicine" (Prov. 17:22). Paul sang in prison. Wesley sang while riding his old horse through a rainstorm in search of a crowd to whom he could preach. Christians today sing in all sorts of circumstances because of the joy that wells up inside and effervesces to the surface. This is nothing that can be faked if it is not there, nothing that can be checked if it is.

Life is a celebration of being alive. God shares His life with these strange creatures called human beings. Even with all of the misery in life, how could we not sing for joy? Well-known heart surgeon Christiaan Barnard wrote of making rounds in a children's hospital when he heard some noise. He looked up to see a breakfast trolley that had been commandeered by two kids. One pushed the cart with his head down, and the other, seated on the lower deck, guided the cart by scraping one foot on the floor.

The boy pushing was blind. His parents had gotten drunk one night and fought. The mother threw a lantern at the father. It missed him and broke over the boy's head and shoulders. The flames blinded him and disfigured him for life. The boy who guided the trolley had recently had his arm and shoulder amputated because of bone cancer. Even so, both of the boys put on quite a show for the other kids in the hospital before the "race" ended in scattered plates and a scolding from the nurses. As Dr. Barnard thought about that experience he wrote:

> Suddenly, I realized that these two children had given me me a profound lesson in getting on with the business of living. Because the business of living is joy in the real sense of the word, not just something

for pleasure, amusement, recreation. *The business of living is the celebration of being alive.*

I had been looking at suffering from the wrong end. You don't become a better person because you are suffering; but you become a better person because you have experienced suffering. We can't appreciate light if we haven't known darkness. Nor can we appreciate warmth if we have never suffered cold. These children showed me that it's not what you've lost that's important. What is important is what you have left.[3]

At one time I was interim pastor of a little church in Kentucky. My first Sunday there I saw that a couple in the community attended worship by the only means of transportation they had—a tractor. The man was blind, so he would sit on a seat especially built for him behind the driver's seat. His wife would drive the old machine to church every Sunday, come rain or shine. It's not what you lost, but what you have left . . .

I see in my memory a woman plagued for twenty years with cancer, tumors that would build up in her stomach, obesity, diabetes, and other problems. But she knew the inner joy of being alive in Christ, and she lived her faith until she died. I miss her because she was my friend. It's not what you lost . . .

A person struggling for his life has little time to fuss about whether he is dressed according to the latest fashion guides. The refusal of us Christians to live in the joy of Christ surely must prompt the tears of God.

Shared Joy

The apostle Paul had been away from his beloved friends, the Thessalonians, and felt the tug of loneliness on his heart. He asked them, "For what is our hope, our joy, or the crown in which we will glory in the presence of our Lord Jesus when he comes? Is it not you? Indeed, you are our glory and joy" (1 Thess. 2:19-20). Paul linked his own eternal joy to his friends. Christian joy is social. People are saved as individuals but always put into a community—the church—to live and work. We are not promised a heaven on earth, in which each does "his own thing," but rather a place where each participates in the life of God. Joy, like life itself, is for sharing.

Paul continued expressing his feelings of this shared experience by stating, "For now we really live, since you are standing firm in the Lord. How can we thank God enough for you in return for all the joy we have in the presence of our God because of you?" (1 Thess. 3:8-9). He spoke, too, of the body of Christ as being made of many parts all joined together: "If one part suffers, every part suffers with it; if one part is honored, every part rejoices with it" (1 Cor. 12:26). Paul knew that the lives of God's people—indeed, *all* people!—are linked together inseparably. In a sense, we are all "Siamese twins" joined at the heart. To separate us is to kill us. As a friend of mine is used to saying, "Well, we'll have to hang together, or we'll all hang separately."

Pearl Bailey, that energetic actress of *Hello Dolly* fame, once remarked that her husband says she worries about people too much. Pearl replied, "I don't worry, I *care*." Exactly! She cares. And people in Christ are called to a life of caring that shares both the pain and the joys of others. This is what helps us live out our lives, lonely though they sometimes may be. In a deep sense we never fully escape the loneliness which seems to surround us like a cloud, and we do not need to escape it. A thoughtful writer reflected on this condition and wrote:

> The Christian way of life does not take away our loneliness; it protects and cherishes it as a precious gift. Sometimes it seems as if we do everything possible to avoid the painful confrontation with our basic human loneliness, and allow ourselves to be trapped by false gods promising immediate satisfaction and quick relief. But perhaps the painful awareness of loneliness is an invitation to transcend our limitations and look beyond the boundaries of our existence. The awareness of loneliness might be a gift we must protect and guard, because our loneliness reveals to us an inner emptiness that can be destructive when misunderstood, but filled with promise for him who can tolerate its sweet pain.[4]

Joy is a fruit of the Spirit. It is shared and helps intensify and transfigure every area of life.

Consider how this happens in your own life. You open the mail and find a card from a friend who has remembered your birthday. You answer the phone and hear the familiar voice of an old acquaintance who is calling to see how you are. You open the door and find a friend you have not seen in a while and whom you have missed. Joy comes in living, and especially in sharing with someone we care about. It comes, too, from reaching out and sharing ourselves with others. After all, *you* are the only gift you have to give away. Rejoice! God has given you life, time, and the gift of joy. As Francis of Assisi put it, "Let us leave sadness to the devil and his angels. As for us, what can we be but rejoicing and glad?"

Finding Joy

Where is joy to be found? If it is a fruit of the Spirit, on what vine does it grow? In whose garden? At the hand of what farmer? People of God through the ages have known that joy comes by knowing the Giver of joy. The psalmist wrote,

> When the LORD brought back the
>   captives to Zion,
>   we were like men who dreamed.
> Our mouths were filled with laughter,
>   our tongues with songs of joy.
> Then it was said among the nations,
>   "The LORD has done great things for
>   them."
> The LORD has done great things for us,
>   and we are filled with joy (Ps. 126:1-3).

God grants such joy as men and women hunger after Him. Again, the psalmist praised the Lord:

> O God, you are my God,
>   earnestly I seek you;
> my soul thirsts for you,
>   my body longs for you,
> in a dry and weary land
>   where there is no water.

....

My soul will be satisfied as with the
richest of foods;
with singing lips my mouth will
praise you (Ps. 63:1;5).

God presents the gift of joy to people who seek *Him* rather than
to those who seek joy. This is partially because joy is gained on the
slant rather than by a frontal assault. Have you ever had trouble going
to sleep? If you lie in bed thinking "I *will* go to sleep! I *will* go to sleep!"
you will probably wake up even more. You do not work at going to
sleep. Instead you relax and let it come. Finding joy is like this, too.

When we seek God, we find Him and His gifts. In finding God, we
are changed, and our thinking and seeing are transformed. The poet
William Blake realized this. He illustrated his work with his own
drawings which he did with a heightened sense of sight. He wrote of
this sight:

> To the eye of a miser a guinea is far more beautiful than the sun and
> a bag worn with the use of money has more beautiful proportions than
> a vine filled with grapes. The tree which moves some to tears of joy is
> in the eyes of others only a green thing which stands in the way. As
> a man is so he sees.
> When the sun rises, do you not see a round disk of fire something
> like a gold piece? O no, no, I see an innumerable company of the
> Heavenly host crying "Holy, Holy, Holy, is the Lord God Almighty."
> I do not question my bodily eye any more than I would question a
> window concerning sight. *I look through it and not with it.*[5]

We find joy—or maybe I should note that joy finds us—as we look
at life through God's eyes. This is never possible in an absolute sense,
but it is in an approximate sense. When I do this I take myself out
of the focus in the center of the picture. Someone else is there, and
once I have gotten outside my own little world I discover the joy of
the rest of God's creation. W. R. Inge wrote about this experience:

> Joy will be ours in so far as we are genuinely interested in great ideas
> outside ourselves. When we have once crossed the charmed circle and
> got outside ourselves, we shall soon realize that all true joy has an

eternal and Divine source and goal. We are immortal spirits, set to do certain things in time; were it not so, our lives would lack any rational justification. The joy of achievement is the recognition of a task understood and done. It is done, and fit to take its place—however lowly a place—in the eternal order. . . . To do our duty in our own sphere, to try to create something worth creating, as our life's work, is the way to understand what joy is in this life, and by God's grace to earn the verdict: "Well done, good and faithful servant; enter thou into the joy of thy Lord."[6]

One who cannot get outside his own skin can never find joy. He or she is too wrapped up in his own tiny universe to be concerned about God or others. When the space shuttle Columbia tragically exploded in January of 1986, the major networks carried the coverage live that day. Local television stations reported being swamped by angry callers who did not want their soap operas interrupted for *any* reason. A secretary at one station tried to explain the tragedy and reported that some responded, "Yes, it is a tragedy all right. I can't watch *As the World Turns.*"[7] How could such people ever hope to experience something as other-centered as joy?

The late L. D. Johnson, long-time chaplain at Furman University, wrote of Jesus that His . . .

happiness corresponded to the universal law that joy comes from self-forgetfulness. The happiest people are the very people who are most interested in other people and are doing most for them. The surest recipe for a joyless, meaningless life is to look at yourself constantly and interpret all reality in terms of how it affects you.[8]

W. B. Wolfe reflected on happiness and realized that joy cannot be chased down like a dollar bill blowing in the wind.

If you observe a really happy man you will find him building a boat, writing a symphony, educating his son, growing double dahlias in his garden . . . He will not be searching for happiness as if it were a collar button that has rolled under the radiator. He will not be striving for it as a goal in itself.[9]

Think of the truly joy-filled people you may know. Aren't they the ones always willing to help others and become involved with them? The ones who spend little or no time complaining about how they feel or that no one calls them or that life has passed them by? God wants this for all His children. The fruit of the Spirit is joy. Why not pick some for yourself as you learn to live for others?

3
The Elusive Butterfly: Peace

Peace is liberty in tranquility.—Cicero

A Jewish friend who grew up in Tel Aviv, Israel, once gave me a gift from his native country—a menorah—the seven-candle holder which is the ancient symbol of peace. Across the front of it is printed the word *shalom*—the Hebrew word for *peace*. Although I have not seen my friend for a long time, his gift is dear to me. It reminds me of our college days together. He was discovering America, struggling with English, and trying to make sense out of Christianity. So was I! This same friend gave me his Israeli "GI" copy of his Bible—an Old Testament written in Hebrew.

A menorah and a Bible—these are powerful reminders of what Paul called one fruit of the Spirit—peace. Peace is like an elusive butterfly we spend our lives chasing but seldom seem to catch. But continue the struggle to gain it we must. As Paul put it, "Let the peace of Christ rule in your hearts" (Col. 3:15a). The strange fact about it, though, is that while we are to be peacemakers, we cannot order a day's supply of peace like we might gather a supply of fire wood. Peace is a gift of God. It cannot be netted but it can be accepted.

Consider Louis Hubert Casebolt. He spent much of his life grabbing after peace for his own purposes, seeking peace as an end in itself.

Seeking Peace for Its Own Sake

The autopsy listed his name as Louis Hubert Casebolt, but for years he was known to his followers as "Archanna Christos" which means the "oldest anointed one."[1] This man had been a spiritual teacher, a former convict, soldier, evangelist, and father of a communal family related by the quest for inner peace. His thirty-year search for inner peace ended when he placed a .22-caliber rifle under his chin and pulled the trigger. His "family" members had given up their former lives in order to share Casebolt's vision. He gave up most material things and modern tools in the search for "intuitive consciousness." The followers of this man lived together in a marsh commune known as Vela Ashby in Plaquemines Parish, Louisiana. The goal was to live off the land and find inner peace through communing with nature.

Casebolt had lived an unusual life. He had gone to prison for manslaughter as a teenager. Later he served as a gunner on a B-17 bomber and was wounded in action during the war. Later he was an evangelist. He gave that up, feeling the thinking of most people was unoriginal and that they were too easily guided by "organized religion" to trouble themselves about inner meaning and peace.

This man's life was tragic on several levels. He began seeking the God of peace but went his own way, hoping to find peace of mind on his own terms. Further, he led others with him in an escape from 'ordinary" living. He finally took his life in what appeared to be a last attempt to find peace, if not in this life, then perhaps in the next.

I respond to this man's life in several directions. First, I am sympathetic with his search, but he went about it wrongfully. Second, I agree with his opinion that too many people simply believe what they are told and do not bother to search out the truth on their own. Mostly, though, I feel compassion for a man who had a rough life and who was never quite able to "put it together." Peace is such an elusive state of mind. It certainly eluded Louis Casebolt.

Even Christians can become trapped in this dead-end grapple for peace for its own sake. Some contemporary Christians tend to take basic religious beliefs and practices and turn them into various expressions of selfishness. Some people declare they read the Bible because it makes them feel good. Reading the Bible certainly can make them feel good, but that is not the paramount reason for digging into the Scriptures. Some churches encourage people to tithe in order to get more from God. That might happen, but stewardship is not a lottery. Some of the most popular religious books emphasize prepackaged ways of making Christianity "work" and gaining personal gratification. Lynn Clayton, editor of the *Baptist Message,* wrote of this trend,

> Don't look for best sellers entitled *Humility—God's Way* or *Serving Others Before Self.* Look for books entitled *God's Way to Financial Abundance* and *How I Prayed Myself Thin.* The way to write a best-selling religious book is to take culture's runaway self-centeredness, wrap it with a thin coat of religious sweetness and give it a catchy title.

What is the answer for such a perversion? Clayton answers:

> We must let the Bible speak in its entirety. We must hear the scriptures proclaim that we find our lives by losing them, and that we are to take up our crosses—and believe that they mean just that. We must stop trying to shape the Bible into some kind of formula-for-personal-success presentation based on religiousized positive thinking. The church must be secure enough in its faith to realize the Gospel will not be popular among all people and that the lowly Galilean was more interested in people's total well-being than just their financial success. The church must emulate the humble spirit and attitude of the Carpenter in all we do.[2]

We can be lulled into thinking that peace is an object or an attitude which can be our private possession if we only search for it enough. We might imagine that peace means we will have no trouble or pain or sorrow. But Jesus was the Prince of peace, and He was nailed to a cross! Peace can be found, even in this strife-wracked world. As Proverbs 14:30 expresses it, "Peace of mind makes the body healthy, but jealousy is like a cancer" (GNB) *Peace comes primarily as a by-product of God's search for us and not primarily by our searching for God and peace themselves.*

I saw a cartoon in which a man walked into a book store. He saw displayed on the shelves books with titles such as *How to Think Right, How to Be Happy, Positive Thinking, The Easy Way, Don't Worry,* and *Mind at Rest.* The customer said to the owner, "Have you got something that won't give me cow-like complacency about the world? I want to be concerned, stimulated, stirred, worried." Closing yourself off from the pain of the rest of the world is no way to find peace.

Searching for the God of Peace

Lord,
Make me an instrument of Thy peace.
Where there is hatred, let me sow love;
Where there is injury, pardon;
Where there is doubt, faith;
Where there is despair, hope;
Where there is darkness, light;
Where there is sadness, joy.
O, Divine Master,
Grant that I may not so much
Seek to be consoled, as to console;
To be understood, as to understand;
To be loved, as to love.
For it is in giving that we receive.
It is in pardoning that we are pardoned.
And it is in dying, that we are born to Eternal life.

The author of that prayer, Francis of Assisi surely understood Jesus' teaching when He taught, "Have salt in yourselves, and be at peace with each other" (Mark 9:50b). Salt is both a preserving and seasoning agent. Peace, like salt, preserves and seasons life. Francis understood this fact.

Solomon, too, knew how to pursue peace. 1 Kings 3 relates how he was told by God to ask for whatever he wanted most. Most people probably would have asked for riches, fame, and long life. But Solomon responded wisely: "Now, O LORD my God, you have made your servant king in place of my father David. But I am only a little child and do not know how to carry out my duties. Your servant is here among the people you have chosen, a great people, too numerous to count or number. So give your servant a discerning heart to govern your people and to distinguish between right and wrong. For who is able to govern this great people of yours?" (1 Kings 3:7-9).

How did God answer? "So God said to him, 'Since you have asked for this and not for long life or wealth for yourself, nor have asked for the death of your enemies but for discernment in administering justice, I will do what you have asked. I will give you a wise and discerning heart, so that there will never have been anyone like you, nor will there ever be" (1 Kings 3:11-12). Solomon got his request, plus more besides, but the point is that he did not ask for selfish things. His request was for the ability to help his people. No wonder his life was peaceful *in the ultimate sense.*

The man or woman who can learn to lean on God and trust in His purposes can learn to receive peace. This is why the Psalmist could write so movingly in Psalm 91:

> He who dwells in the shelter of the
>   Most High
> will rest in the shadow of the
>   Almighty.
> I will say of the LORD, "He is my
>   refuge and my fortress,
> My God, in whom I trust."
> Surely he will save you from the
>   fowler's snare
> and from the deadly pestilence.
> He will cover you with his feathers,
>   and under his wings you will find refuge;
> his faithfulness will be your shield and rampart.
> You will not fear the terror of night,
>   nor the arrow that flies by day,
> nor the pestilence that stalks in the darkness,
>   nor the plague that destroys at midday.
> A thousand may fall at your side,
>   ten thousand at your right hand,
>   but it will not come near you (Ps. 91:1-7).

How well we would sleep if we could pray such a prayer each evening!

Finding the Peace of God

Peace, that elusive butterfly, seems always ready to flap its wings and flutter out of reach. You grab for it, but it eludes you. Do not give up in despair. Instead, allow it to come to you. The peace which God gives is the deepest and most satisfying we may know. There are several things we can do to get it. Let me suggest a few.

We must learn to seek and cultivate silence at times. For whatever reason, God does not like to shout over the roar of our lives. How noisy our lives are! How incessant they are! My twin sons, Ryan and Chris, are five. They are normal, healthy boys in constant overdrive. Finding times of quiet around our house is difficult, but finding it is even more essential because of the usual chaos. Sometimes I must still the external and internal noises so I can listen for God.

Think of the noises in your life that disturb peace. The alarm clock buzzes the blissful dreams out of your head. The children are grumpy. Your spouse is not little Miss (or Mr.) Sunshine. You poured the wrong cereal for one kid, and the other can't find his shoes. You are late for work, and voices rise in direct proportion to the number of minutes you are behind. Traffic is crazy and congested and the office or factory or school is no better. People pull at you all day, the phone never seems to stop ringing, and one hassle after another seems to have your name on it. When quitting time comes you are worn to the proverbial frazzle. You would like nothing better than to lie back in your favorite chair for an hour and regroup the internal forces. But there are traffic to fight, kids to pick up, the PTA meeting, the choir practice, the car that needs realigning, the dishes that need washing, the beds that need changing. Whew! How can you find silence in a life like that?

Getting up a little earlier or going to bed a little later is one way to find a few extra minutes. Learning to use travel time for prayer and Bible "listening" is helpful. Invest in a copy of the New Testament on cassette and listen to it, if possible, while you travel. Listening lends a different dimension from reading. If you are married, perhaps rearranging the household schedule and duties can free up a little time for personal reflection and quietness.

Psalm 131 has only three verses, but they are powerful:

> My heart is not proud, O LORD,
>   my eyes are not haughty;
> I do not concern myself with great matters
>   or things too wonderful for me.
> *But I have stilled and quieted my soul;*

> like a weaned child with its mother,
> like a weaned child is my soul
> within me.
> O Israel, put your hope in the LORD
> both now and forevermore (Italics added).

"I have stilled and quieted my soul." Those words cut right through me because they remind me how vital this is to my well-being. Even Jesus found that He had to withdraw to quiet places for times of reflection and prayer. If He needed it, what about us?

Some of you reading these words have the opposite problem from what I am describing. For you life is already quiet—too quiet. You might be single or widowed. You would give anything for some excitement, some tension, some noise. A married friend of mine, who because of physical problems can never have a child, was visiting in our home recently. My wife and I were apologizing for the noisiness of our boys, and I said, "There are times I would give anything for an hour of absolute silence." This friend looked at me and said, "And there are times when I would give anything for an hour of laughing children." Our boys have adopted this girl as their special friend. Her name is Anna, and they refer to her as "our Anna." We all love her dearly.

There are many Anna's, or Bill's for that matter, who are living lives which are too quiet, and seem at times devoid of some of the richness which life has to offer. To them—to you reading this if you are one such person—I say that your condition can give you special access to the deep things of the Spirit which the rest of us may not know. The slower pace and less distracted nature of your circumstances can allow you to commune with the God of peace. You may know an inner peace which is beyond what many people who seem to have everything will ever know. As Paul once put it, "I have learned the secret of being content in any and every situation" (Phil. 4:12*a*).

Another way to gain the peace of God is to avoid those things which war against peace, and seek those which lead to it. All of us, no matter how strong we might be, are influenced by our surroundings and by other people. A child who grows up in home where chaos and anger reign begins with two strikes against him. A young person whose friends are evil-minded troublemakers has a very tough time breaking free of such influence in order to live for Christ. A person who works with associates who think that life is nothing but *bon temp roulette* —let the good times roll—will have to work doubly hard to find the peace which Paul describes as part of the fruit of the Spirit.

This problem has always existed. Consider the dilemma of the man described in Psalm 120:4-6:

> Woe to me that I dwell in Meshech,
>> that I live among the tents of Kedar!
> Too long have I lived
>> among those who hate peace.
> I am a man of peace;
>> but when I speak, they are for war.

I know how he felt. I, too, "live among the tents of Kedar," among those who are aggressive and pugnacious. I, too, live among those who are always talking about showing someone—whether it be an individual or another nation—how "tough" they are. Unfortunately, this is not all just talk, but is action, too. In 1985 world military spending was $800 billion. This was $60 billion more than just one year earlier. The United States and the Soviet Union, with only about 11 percent of the world's population, spent more than half of that $800 billion total. Annual per capita military spending among the United States and its European allies amounted to about $45, compared with $11 for health research. Overall, the world spends about $450 to educate each child and $25,600 to support each soldier.[4]

How can we allow such an imbalance? Have our priorities for peace not been hijacked? Consider this, too. In 1984 businesses in the United States spend $23 billion just on advertising! This is more than the annual budgets of 130 entire nations of the world.[5] Do we really need to have more and more toothpaste pushed down our throats by the whiz kids of Madison Avenue? Men, women, and children of peace cry out to God that we might regain some sense of fairness and equality about us. Jesus came as the "Prince of peace." It is not that he gave in and backed off from every challenge. In fact, he faced each one. He challenged the warmongers by being a tough-minded peacemaker. He calls his followers to be people of peace, even if it costs them everything. How difficult this is! Someone spoke about this matter this way:

> All too often, we Christians seek "peace"—the sticky unloving kind that has as its goal only our own freedom from discomfort or danger. Our Lord is the Prince of Peace, who always seeks the true peace even at the cost of disturbing the peace. And today he asks the same of all who aspire to be his followers.[6]

Near the old provincial capital of Ou Dong in Cambodia the countryside is littered with empty bullet shells. These are the leftovers of a civil war that ravaged the country many years ago. Children find these spent shells and take them to local foundries where they are melted down and recast as bells to be hung on the necks of oxen. Where once the brass was the casings for shells and destruction, it is now the means of the gentle ringing of bells as the Cambodians go about their work.[7]

From shells to bells—this is the hope of all who follow the master of peace. It is the "swords to plowshares" dream of Isaiah, and the "Day of the Lord" hope of Joel. But how does this hope become reality for Christians today? It comes through our participation in the cross of Christ. Paul said it this way:

> May I never boast except in the cross of our Lord Jesus Christ, through which the world has been crucified to me, and I to the world. Neither circumcision nor uncircumcision means anything; what counts is a new creation. Peace and mercy to all who follow this rule, even to the Israel of God (Gal. 6:14-16).

Paul promised the peace of God to those who participate in the life of Christ by being crucified to the world, and it to them. This does not mean literal death, but rather putting to death those attitudes and actions which ruin the prospects of living God's reality. In other words, I cannot pray and hope for peace if I am unwilling to get out of the rat-race of competition and self promotion. Peace will indeed be the "elusive butterfly" until I am re-molded into the likeness of Christ. (Phil. 2:5-11) Even then, Christ's peace will be vastly different from simple freedom from discomfort or annoyance. That is not peace anyway—it is boredom!

Many years ago a document was written, exuding the sort of wisdom which can lead to peace. Consider the counsel of the "Desiderata."

Go placidly amid the noise and haste, and remember what peace there may be in silence. As far as possible without surrender be on good terms with all persons. Speak your truth quietly and clearly; and listen to others, even the dull and ignorant; they too have their story.

Avoid loud and aggressive persons; they are vexations to the spirit. If you compare yourself with others, you may become vain and bitter; for always there will be greater and lesser persons than yourself. Enjoy your achievements as well as your plans.

Keep interested in your own career, however humble; it is a real possession in the changing fortunes of time. Exercise caution in your business affairs; for the world is full of trickery. But let this not blind you to what virtue there is; many persons strive for high ideals; and everywhere life is full of heroism.

Be yourself. Especially, do not feign affection. Neither be cynical about love; for in the face of all aridity and disenchantment it is a perennial as the grass.

Take kindly the counsel of the years, gracefully surrendering the things of youth. Nurture strength of spirit to shield you in sudden misfortune. But do not distress yourself with imaginings. Many fears are born of fatigue and loneliness. Beyond a wholesome discipline be gentle with yourself.

You are a child of the universe, no less than the trees and the stars; you have a right to be here. And whether or not it is clear to you, no doubt the universe is unfolding as it should.

Therefore be at peace God, whatever you conceive Him to be; and whatever your labors and aspirations, in the noisy confusion of life keep peace with your soul.

With all its sham, drudgery, and broken dreams, it is still a beautiful world. Be careful. Strive to be happy.

I would not agree with all the sentiments of this document, but it is nonetheless helpful to me as I try to pick this fruit of the Spirit— peace. This is a virtue of grace that cannot be captured by force but can be lured by love. What are you using for bait?

4
Hang On and Hold Out— Patience

Patience, that blending of moral courage with physical timidity.—Thomas Hardy

The nine-millimeter automatic pistol was buried deeply into the back of his neck as the wild-eyed men shouted, "Hijack! Hijack!" With this incident a grueling seventeen-day hijacking of TWA Flight 847 began for Captain John Testrake and his crew on June 14, 1985. What was supposed to be a normal short hop from Athens, Greece, to Rome, Italy, ended up being nearly a three-week test of wills for two Shiite Moslem hijackers and two Christian jet pilots.

The incident ended and Captain Testrake, along with Flight Engineer Christian Zimmermann, finally came home. Testrake later told of the days of captivity and the uncertainty of ever seeing freedom again. He remembered how his first wife died of cancer and how his oldest son died suddenly at the age of twenty-seven. Even with all those painful memories and the fear of being hijacked, Testrake testified of his experience, "I remember the constant presence of Jesus. He kept me from being afraid. He comforted me. He gave me hope. He gave me freedom, though I was a captive. And He is with me still as I continue to fly for TWA."[1]

How does one under constant threat of death hold out? How does the mother of a physically handicapped child keep going and refuse to give up? How does a man with a sour job find the strength to go to work every day instead of quitting and letting his family go hungry? How do people living in poverty find the inner courage to keep struggling in order to do the best they can? The answer is—"patience."

Patience—in the Christian sense—is not sitting idly by while the world goes on. It is not even wishful thinking. Patience, as a fruit of the Spirit, is the deep, personal knowledge that God is working in

47

your life and in His world. This knowledge allows a hijack victim to hold out until the end. It allows the mother of a handicapped child to keep working and doing the best she can. It helps the man with a job that is not so great to go on with the job without investing all his hopes and dreams in the business. Patience has been defined as "living out the belief that God orders everything for the spiritual good of his children. Patience does not just grin and bear things, stoic-like, but accepts them cheerfully as therapeutic workouts planned by a heavenly trainer who is resolved to get you up to full fitness."[2]

But this is obviously easier said than done! It is one matter to accept such a definition mentally, but another thing altogether to accept it emotionally. We do not live out of definitions but out of that complex interrelation of mind, body, and spirit. Our bodies, for example, might seem to be in open revolt against us, but still the mind and spirit can overcome all resistance and end up serving a loving Heavenly Father. This takes patience, which is active participation in the will of God, and not just passive waiting.

A well-known writer put it like this: "The Christian patience is not a grim, bleak acceptance of a situation; even the patience is irradiated with joy. *The Christian waits, not as one who waits for the night, but as one who waits for the morning.*"[3]

I am reminded of a line from one of Gilbert and Sullivan's operas: "Do you know what it is to seek oceans and find puddles?" I answer that question, "Yes! I do." And I suppose you do, too. We want so much. We want good things, even great things, not in the sense of possessions, but quality of life and mind. But we find that we cannot have everything we desire. Life seems rather fizzled out at times, and each day seems a carbon copy of the one before it. How do we deal with the puddles when we are taught to seek oceans? The answer is: through that strength of inner life which the Bible calls patience. This comes from a God who is patient.

The Patience of God

Older versions of the Bible call patience "long suffering." That is a highly descriptive term that is used even of God. I sometimes wonder what life would be like if God were like me—or anyone else, for that matter. How would He relate to the world? If God were like me He would have tired of the whole swampy mess a long time ago, and would have destroyed it. Thank heaven God is not like you or me.

The prophet Jeremiah gives us a picture of God's patience. Jeremiah went to a potter's house and watched him working at his wheel. "But the pot he was shaping from the clay was marred in his hands; so the potter formed it into another pot, shaping it as seemed best to him. Then the word of the LORD came to me: 'O house of Israel, can I not do with you as this potter does?' declares the LORD. Like clay in the hand of the potter, so are you in my hand O house of Israel" (Jer. 18:4-6). This is a powerful image. It tells us that God has in mind a design and a goal for people. God keeps moving us toward this goal and design. He is the patient Potter Who shapes and forms and molds the clay. Even when it gets marred in His hand He does not throw it away but reshapes it.

The Old Testament affirms the patience of God toward people. Exodus 34:6-7 states, "And he [God] passed in front of Moses, proclaiming, 'The LORD, the LORD, the compassionate God, slow to anger, abounding in love and faithfulness, maintaining love to thousands, and forgiving wickedness and rebellion and sin.' " The second half of verse 7 puts this patience in perspective, however: "Yet he does not leave the guilty unpunished." God is no tottering, senile being who sits in his heavenly rocking chair, allowing people to do whatever they wish! He is "slow to anger" because he wants people to change, and God knows that change is not easy.

Nehemiah referred to his spiritual ancestors in Israel and prayed to the Lord, "But you are a forgiving God, gracious and compassionate, slow to anger and abounding in love. Therefore you did not desert them" (Neh. 9:17b). The Psalms echo this assessment about God. Psalm 86:15 sounds nearly like Nehemiah: "But you, O Lord, are a compassionate and gracious God, slow to anger, abounding in love and faithfulness." Psalm 103:8 says, "The LORD is compassionate and gracious, slow to anger, abounding in love." Psalm 145:8 declares: "The LORD is gracious and compassionate, slow to anger and rich in love."

This sounds like good news, but at least one person in the Old Testament did not like God's patience. That one person was Jonah. He went as a reluctant missionary to Nineveh to preach repentance, and to his great surprise—and regret!—the people repented. God was good to His promise not to destroy them, and Jonah did not like that one bit. Chapter 4 of Jonah begins: "But Jonah was greatly displeased and became angry. He prayed to the LORD, 'O LORD, is this not what I said when I was still at home? That is why I was so quick to flee to Tarshish. I knew that you are a gracious and compassionate God, slow to anger and abounding in love, a God who relents from sending calamity. Now, O LORD, take away my life, for it is better for me to die than to live.' " To this whining of Jonah God asks one question: "Have you any right to be angry?" The implied answer was, of course, no.

The New Testament states even clearer that God is patient with His strange creation called human beings. Paul spoke of himself as the worst of sinners, a blasphemer and a persecutor. But God was patient with him in order to save him. "But for that very reason I was shown mercy so that in me, the worst of sinners, Christ Jesus might display his unlimited patience as an example for those who would believe on him and receive eternal life" (1 Tim. 1:16). Peter also affirmed the patience of God that leads to salvation: "The Lord is not slow in keeping his promise, as some understand slowness. He is patient with you, not wanting anyone to perish, but everyone to come to repentance" (2 Pet. 3:9). Peter also said of this, "Bear in mind that our Lord's patience means salvation, just as our dear brother Paul also wrote you with the wisdom that God gave him" (2 Pet. 3:15).

God waits with a holy patience for people to come to their senses and give their lives to Him. He waits for people to come alive to the possibilities of living in union with Him. He waits as people wear out many a hammer against the anvil of his patience, and finally realize that they are His, no matter what. God waits on us.

And we wait on God. I do not mean anything sacrilegious with this statement. What I do mean is that patience is required on our part as we work to understand God more fully and to live in that understanding. Do you know everything about God? Do you fully understand His ways? Of course not! And neither does anyone else. I often wonder about God's way in the world. I cannot comprehend it fully, so I must live with an assurance that it is all combining and interacting for the good of those who love Him (Rom. 8:28). God does things which I might not do if the choice were mine. But thank the Lord, He does not need my permission to do what He knows is the best.

The movie *Amadeus* presents Wolfgang Amadeus Mozart as a "superlatively gifted jerk."[4] He used his brilliant mind to create the most inspiring and uplifting music of his age, and of any age. But Mozart was a base, profane man, at least in the film version of his life. Another composer in the movie was Antonio Salieri. Salieri was a so-so composer with ordinary talents, but he was sharp enough to appreciate Mozart's genius. What Salieri could not understand is why God chose to put such gifts into such a person as Mozart. Someone wrote of this:

> Salieri had ached for a sublime talent that would reflect back to God the effulgence of the divine beauty and simultaneously make the reflector celebrated and immortal. Salieri, that is, had run for election as the voice of God. God's response was to place his treasure in an obscene brat. Thus the musical incarnation of the glory of God ("Amadeus" means, of course, beloved of God) prances through the film with a . . . grin on his face. . . .[5]

Situations like this exist, usually in lesser ways, for all Christians. We do not know why some people seem to have ten talents while others have only one or two. We need patience to live with the realization that God does not consult with us before giving his gifts. One of the great mysteries is that God's best gift, His Son, was born in a stable with its numbing dampness and smell of cattle dung. How the gift and the container were unmatched! God gives all things to those who live in Him and wait. As Paul put it, "If God is for us, who can be against us? He who did not spare his own Son, but gave him up for us all—how will he not also, along with him, graciously give us all things?" (Rom. 8:31*a*-32).

Cultivating the Art of Patient Living

Patience is the God-given power of creative waiting. This is far different from twiddling your thumbs while resting in your favorite recliner and hoping your lot improves. The Spirit of God gives patience as part of His fruit. It is therefore to be cultivated, tended, cared for, valued, and protected.

Waiting is one thing, but *creative* waiting is quite another. This is the hard task of life navigation. You want to do something, make a career change for example, but find that you cannot do it now. Several possibilities are open to you. 1. You could sit around and bemoan the job you have now, and berate everyone associated with it. But all this will do is make you more miserable and hurt you by making you continually angry. 2. Another option is to tell the boss off and quit tomorrow. But the bills will still show up in the mail box with frightening regularity, so this will not do. 3. Another possibility is to focus your energy and attention in another direction to things which attract you. For example, a person who is a secretary and bored with her job might spend her off duty time studying to become a real estate agent. This is creative waiting. It is being willing to do one thing for a while—in this example, staying with the secretarial job—until something better can be entered—namely, the real estate position.

Parents of small children learn this kind of patience. They are willing to put up with cereal on the ceiling and marbles in the bathtub drain because they hope something better will come. My wife and I are parents of twin boys who are four and one half at this writing. We have really learned from our twins. Ryan is at a stage where he wants to wear the same pair of shorts every day, and we have a continual struggle about his appearance. Chris has learned a strange trick of tucking the top portion of his right ear into the ear canal so it sticks there. People who do not know him feel sorry for this "deformed" little boy.

I do not have all the friends I want but am continually coming into contact with people who are potential friends. One problem is when some people learn I am a minister they feel distance from me. Ministers—so some people seem to think—are not human and do not want or need friendship! I am not sure what we preachers have done to warrant such an idea. I cannot speak about my colleagues, but I for one desire and need friendship. So for me, patience is that creative waiting as people come to know me as "a real live human being" with troubles of my own, bills to pay, and a sense of humor.

My favorite comic strip is Gary Larson's "The Far Side." I have several of the books in which these cartoons are collected, and they give me great belly laughs. I shared these with some of the members of a class I lead, and before long word had spread throughout the congregation that the preacher has a weird sense of humor. People were helped to see me as a unique person rather than a stiff, cold-blooded "parson." I have waited long for this change in perception. [By the way, the members read and enjoyed "The Far Side" books, too.]

John Chrysostom was a leader in the early church. He lived from about AD 347 until 407. He once spoke on patience in a powerful manner:

> for it is both an invincible weapon and a sort of impregnable tower, easily beating off all annoyances: and as a spark falling into the keep doth it no injury, but is itself easily quenched, so whatever unexpected thing falls upon a long-suffering soul speedily vanishes, but the soul it disturbs not; for of a truth there is nothing so impenetrable as long-suffering. You may talk of armies, money, horses, walls, arms, or anything else, you will name nothing like long-suffering; for he that is surrounded by these, being overcome by anger, is upset, like a worthless child, and fills all with confusion and tempest; but the long-suffering man, settled as it were in a harbour, enjoys a profound calm. Though he may be surrounded with loss, the rock is not moved; though thou bruise him with stripes, thou hast not wounded the adamant. The possessor of this passive virtue hath a kind of long and noble soul, whose great strength is love.[6]

Patience does indeed make a "noble soul." As James puts it, "Consider it pure joy, my brothers, whenever you face trials of many kinds, because you know that the testing of your faith develops perseverance. Perseverance must finish its work so that you may be mature and complete, not lacking anything" (James 1:2-3). The ability to wait creatively is part of God's plan for us, because we learn so much in the process.

James also spoke of patience as we wait for the Lord's return. Listen to his counsel: "Be patient, then, brothers, until the Lord's coming. See how the farmer waits for the land to yield its valuable crop and how patient he is for the fall and spring rains. You too, be patient and stand firm, because the Lord's coming is near." (Jas. 5:7-8).

This kind of patience is certainly not meant to make you stale. It is not intended to lead to dry rot or decay. People, like fine silverware, stay in the best shape with constant use; otherwise, both tend to tarnish. Thomas Hardy's old novel, *The Mayor of Casterbridge,* gives this description of a young married couple walking down a road together, while the woman held an infant: "That the man and woman were husband and wife and the parents of the girl in arms there could be little doubt. No other than such relationship would have accounted for the atmosphere of stale familiarity which the trio carried with them . . . as they moved down the road." "The atmosphere of stale familiarity"—this is such a sad description. This is not what biblical patience produces. Creative waiting is not merely putting up with bad situations, but it is learning and growing from them. Shortly before he died, Ulysses S. Grant wrote a note to his doctor. It read, "The fact is that I think I am a verb instead of a personal pronoun. A verb is anything that signifies to be; to do; or to suffer. I signify all three."[7] I have no idea if Grant were a patient man, but his note captured a portion of Christian patience in the sense of speaking about life as being active in some parts while waiting in others.

The apostle Paul probably wrote his letter to the Ephesians from a prison cell. You would think he would have been angry, bitter, resentful, and nearly dying to get out. But consider his counsel to the Ephesians: "As a prisoner for the Lord, then, I urge you to live a life worthy of the calling you have received. Be completely humble and gentle; be patient, bearing with one another in love. Make every effort to keep the unity of the Spirit through the bond of peace" (Eph. 4:1-3). Can you imagine a prisoner telling free people to be patient? It seems laughable, but Paul could do this, because at the deepest level, he too was free. His soul, his mind, and his imagination were all free. Only his body was captive. Paul lived patience as creative waiting. If he could not visit his friends in Ephesus, at least he could write.

Think of this for a while. You cannot do everything you want to. (If you can, then you have your sights set too low!) But you can do so many other things. Perhaps like Paul you need to begin doing what you *can* do instead of fretting over what you *cannot* do. Maybe you need to write or call some people who need to hear from you, and/or you need to practice the art of creative waiting by volunteering some of your time to vital church or community activities while you anticipate other developments. The writer of Hebrews admonished, "We do not want you to become lazy, but to imitate those who through faith and patience inherit what has been promised" (Heb. 6:12).

Patience is the power to accept life's hard knocks without falling apart. Every person is caught in circumstances he did not choose. Every person has problems she would rather do without. But life is no cafeteria line where we choose only what sounds good.

The inability to accept life leads mental distress in the highest order. Ty Cobb was a legendary baseball player. He had a lifetime batting average of .367. He stole 892 bases, had 4,191 hits, and scored 2,245 runs from 1905 until 1928. It sounds like Cobb "had it made." But a sports writer recently summed up Cobb's life:

> His talents for collecting base hits was equaled only by a perverted genius for alienating people. So to hear Cobb described by his peers as the game's greatest player is a most telling tribute, because most of the encomiasts despised him, usually with evidence in hand, because Ty at one time or another had spiked them, turned them down, slugged them, bedeviled them, insulted them, or otherwise unsettled their digestive tracts.[8]

Two of his sons, Ty, Jr., and Herschel, died before Cobb. At the age of seventy-one Cobb tried to move back to his old home near Cornelia, Georgia. He wanted to settle down but could not. He criss-crossed the country several more times searching for peace and happiness, but he never found it. Cobb apparently could not accept life with its family tragedies.

I am sympathetic with Cobb and with the millions of people like him. They spend a lifetime running and searching for the "something" which is hard to describe, but they never find it. These people do not know the power of creative waiting which the Bible calls patience.

John Milton, the English master of the sonnet (1608-1674), wrote a poem on his blindness. The last line has become familiar to many people, but the entire poem speaks of patience.

> When I consider how my light is spent
>> Ere half my days in this dark world and wide,
>> And that one talent which is death to hide
>> Lodged with me useless, though my soul more bent
> To serve therewith my Maker, and present
>> My true account, lest He returning chide,
>> "Doth God exact day-labour, light denied?"
>> I fondly ask. But Patience, to prevent
> That murmur, soon replies, "God doth not need
>> Either man's work or his own gifts. Who best
>> Bear his mild yoke, they serve him best. His state
> Is kingly: thousands at his bidding speed,
>> And post o'er land and ocean without rest;
>> They also serve who only stand and wait."

Sometimes all we can do is "stand and wait." But Milton was right. That, too, can be service to God. Isaiah tells us: "They who wait for the LORD shall renew their strength" (Isa. 40:31, RSV). The word *wait* here means to "twist together as a rope." Isaiah indicates that those who intertwine their lives with the life of God are strengthened. This, certainly, is patience as creative waiting.

I end this chapter with an ancient story about a rabbi named Hillel. He lived about BC 20 and was considered the most patient of all the teachers at that time. Two men made a wager to the effect that whoever could make Hillel angry and lose his patience would receive four hundred *Zuz.* So one of the men boasted, "I will make him angry."

It was Sabbath eve, and Hillel was washing his hair. The man went to Hillel's house and shouted at the door, "Is Hillel in? Is Hillel in?" Hillel dressed himself and asked the man, "What do you wish, my son?" The man answered, "I wish to ask you a question." "You may ask it, my son," replied Hillel. "Why are the heads of Babylonians round?" "You have asked a great question, my son," answered Hillel. "Because the midwives of the Babylonians are not very experienced."

The man waited an hour, came back, and shouted, "Is Hillel in? Is Hillel in?" Hillel dressed again and went out to him: "What do you wish, my son?" "I wish to ask a question." "Ask, my son." "Why are the eyes of the Tadmorenes (natives of Palmyra) inflamed?" "You have asked a great question," replied Hillel. "Because they live in sandy places."

The man waited another hour, went back, and again shouted, "Is Hillel in? Is Hillel in?" Hillel dressed again and went out to him. "What do you wish, my son?" "I have a question to ask." "Ask, my son," replied the rabbi. "Why are the feet of the Africans broad?" "You have asked a great question, my son," answered Hillel. "Because they live in watery marshes." Then the man said, "I have many questions to ask you but fear that you will become angry." Whereupon Hillel adjusted his robes, sat down near him, and said, "Ask all the questions you have to ask."

Then the man inquired, "Are you Hillel that is prince of Israel? If it is you, then there should be no more men like you in Israel." "Why?" asked Hillel. "Because I lost four hundred *Zuz* because of you." Hillel said, "Be careful of your temper. Hillel is worth the loss of four hundred *Zuz* and many times four hundred; but you cannot make Hillel lose his patience."[9]

Learning patience is always costly. It costs a life given to Christ for the grafting in of this fruit of the Spirit. Got the time?

5
Ethics of the Second Mile— Kindness

The greatest thing a man can do for his Heavenly Father is to be kind to some of His other children.—Henry Drummond.

Before becoming a Christian, Martin of Tours had been a Roman cavalry officer. One winter he was riding with his regiment through the snow and slush into the city of Amiens. Crowds gathered to watch the nearly-frozen soldiers coming in. As it passed through the city, the young officer Martin dismounted. He had seen among the crowd a poor man, almost naked, blue with cold, holding out his trembling hand for alms to buy bread. Martin removed his own cloak, cut it in two, and then wrapped half of it around the shivering shoulders of the begger. He put the other half around himself, then remounted, and rode off.

That night as he slept he dreamed of the half coat and heard a voice asking him if he had ever seen it. Martin looked at it, expecting to see the begger whom he had befriended earlier that day. He saw no beggar, but only the strong, gracious face and form of Jesus. As he stared at the vision, the crowd of peasants who had laughed at his gesture toward the beggar seemed to change into groups of the heavenly host.

Martin of Tours learned the truth of Jesus' statement regarding kind acts, "When you have done it unto one of these, the least of my brethren, you have done it unto me." A seemingly extravagant act of kindness led to a life-changing encounter between God and Martin. But this is not so unusual because similar events have happened with many people. Paul urged the Christian church in Colosse to wrap kindness around them as a cloak: "As God's chosen people, holy and dearly loved, clothe yourselves with compassion [and] kindness" (Col. 3:12).

This council might seem like the proverbial "fiddling while Rome burns." Can you imagine saying to the president of Libya, "Now, Mr. Moammar Gadhafi, you must be kind"? Or can you picture someone telling the ruler of Iran, "Remember now, Sir, you are supposed to act with kindness"? That some would consider kindness a dispensible notion is perfectly obvious. But that kindness was considered by Jesus of Nazareth an absolute necessity is equally obvious.

Jesus urged His followers, "If someone wants to sue you for your tunic, let him have your cloak as well. If someone forces you to go one mile, go with him two miles" (Matt. 5:40-41). "Going the extra mile" is a phrase that has gained general usage in our society. It signifies doing more than is required, of exceeding the minimum. *Kindness is the ethic of the second mile.* It is the willingness to do more for others than might be required in any given circumstance. As such, it is the basis for all strong and healthy relationships.

The Kindness of God

The Bible proclaims that God is *for* people. Paul expressed this idea: "For the Son of God, Jesus Christ, who was preached among you by me and Silas and Timothy, was not 'Yes' and 'No,' but in him it has always been 'Yes.' For no matter how many promises God has made, they are 'Yes' in Christ" (2 Cor. 1:19-20). Consider that. God says "Yes" to us! Out of His eternal kindness, God really loves us and affirms us. That is gospel—supreme good news.

In another place Paul spoke of the tremendous mercy of God toward people: "But because of his great love for us, God, who is rich in mercy, made us alive with Christ even when we were dead in transgressions—it is by grace you have been saved. And God raised us up with Christ and seated us with him in the heavenly realms in Christ Jesus, in order that in the coming ages he might show the incomparable riches of his grace, expressed in his kindness to us in Christ Jesus" (Eph. 2:4-7). Paul knew of God's kindness, but he never thought of it as indulgence or apathy on God's part. He warned the Christians in Rome to consider together both the sternness and kindness of God (see Rom. 11:11-24).

Isaiah had proclaimed this good news, too. He spoke of God's touching compassion upon His people:

> I will tell of the kindnesses of the
> LORD,
>> the deeds for which he is to be
>> praised,
>> according to all the LORD had done
>> for us—
> yes, the many good things he has
> done
>> for the house of Israel,
>> according to his compassion and
>> many kindnesses (Isa. 63:7).

Isaiah had wrestled all his life to understand God. He had known the power, the majesty, the strength, but he also came to know the kindness. The Old Testament understanding of this aspect of God's character is unique. Other religions of the ancient Near East conceived of many kinds of gods, such as Isis and Ra. These religions thought of their deities as capricious, fickle, or even untrustworthy, but the Bible calls the Lord a God Who is kind.

This kindness was why God could forgive and lead His people back to Himself. The prophet Nehemiah spoke of the history of his people as they would forsake God, fall into difficulty, repent, and then be brought back to Him. "And when they cried out to you again, you heard from heaven, and in your compassion you delivered them time after time" (Neh. 9:28b). This aspect of "time after time" sounds like my own life. Does it sound like yours? I "work hard" at living for God and doing what I pray is right. Then when things are going smoothly, like the ancient Hebrews, I slack off. I fall into difficulty and then turn with renewed vigor to God. Thank the Lord, He hears and accepts me back into full fellowship.

The kindness of God thus leads to restored relationships. The Psalmist prayed, "Remember, O LORD, your great mercy and love, for they are from of old. Remember not the sins of my youth and my rebellious ways; according to your love remember me, for you are good, O LORD" (Ps. 25:6-7). God sent his Son to restore relationships which had been broken because of sin. The meaning of the Incarnation is that God wanted to bring people back to himself.

Think of the kindness Jesus showed people. It ranged from a general compassion for many to specific kind acts toward individuals. When He went into towns and villages teaching and preaching He was emotionally moved by what He found. Matthew tells us, "When he saw the crowds, he had compassion on them, because they were harassed and helpless, like sheep without a shepherd" (Matt. 9:36). The unfortunate were special recipients of Jesus' care.

Two blind men sat by the roadside on one occasion when Jesus passed by and called out for healing. Matthew says, "Jesus had compassion on them and touched their eyes. Immediately they received their sight and followed him" (Matt. 20:34). Many bereaved people experienced Christ's special kindness. A mother was walking in a funeral procession when Jesus approached. Luke relates the incident: "When the Lord saw her, his heart went out to her and he said, 'Don't cry.' Then he went up and touched the coffin, and those carrying it stood still. He said, 'Young man, I say to you, get up!' The dead man sat up and began to talk, and Jesus gave him back to his mother" (Luke 7:13-15).

Many children know that John 11:35 is the shortest verse in the Bible—"Jesus wept." Its main significance is not its length but the picture it paints of Jesus. He *cared.* He cared about the relationship He had with His friend Lazarus and was grieved at his death. The next verse says, "Then the Jews said, 'See how he loved him!' " He cared about the sisters of Lazarus and so raised him from the dead because they depended on him.

Once Jesus felt the pain of a city that would not heed his message. "O Jerusalem, Jerusalem, you who kill the prophets and stone those sent to you, how often I have longed to gather your children together, as a hen gathers her chicks under her wings, but you were not willing" (Matt. 23:37). No one can doubt the love, compassion, and kindness of one so deeply moved by the plight of others.

Kindness Toward Others

God is kind and expects His people to show a similar attitude toward others. Some anonymous author observed:

> The ministry of kindness is a ministry which may be achieved by all men, rich and poor, learned and illiterate. Brilliance of mind and capacity for deep thinking have rendered great service to humanity, but by themselves they are impotent to dry a tear or mend a broken heart.

The Bible is rich with this same sentiment and proclaims this ethic of the second mile. Kindness is expressed through the words which we speak. Words are powerful and have the power to hurt or to heal. Proverbs 15:4 goes, "Kind words bring life, but cruel words crush your spirit" (GNB). Verse 23 states, "What a joy it is to find just the right word for the right occasion!" One simple act of kindness that can be shown toward others is to speak to them with soothing, caring words. Have you noticed how touchy most people seem? They are apparently hassled by others and begin to view every person as a potential enemy. The next time you are in a checkout line with a harried clerk, speak a kind word and see what happens. Sometimes these simple, almost casual acts of kindness affect people deeply and significantly. Oscar Wilde was an author in Victorian England whose actions matched his name. He was sent to prison for two years for a sexual crime and was later converted to Christian faith. He wrote of an incident that happened during part of his trial that changed his life.

> When I was brought down from my prison to the Court of Bankruptcy, between two policemen, _____ waited in the long dreary corridor that, before the whole crowd, whom an action so sweet and simple hushed into silence, he might gravely raise his hat to me, as, handcuffed and with bowed head, I passed him by. . . . It was in this spirit, and with this mode of love, that the saints knelt down to wash the feet of the poor, or stooped to kiss the leper on the cheek. I have never said one single word to him about what he did. I do not know to the present moment whether he is aware that I was even conscious of his action. It is not a thing for which one can render formal thanks in formal words. I store it in the treasure-house of my heart. I keep it there as a secret debt that I am glad to think I can never possibly repay.

> . . . *When wisdom has been profitless to me, philosophy barren, and the proverbs and phrases of those who have sought to give me consolation as dust and ashes in my mouth, the memory of that little, lovely silent act of love has unsealed for me all the wells of pity, . . . and brought me out of the bitterness of lonely exile into harmony with the wounded, broken, and great heart of the world.*[1]

The tipping of a hat as an act of kindness—isn't that a strange act to remember? Not really! Most of us remember these little things when someone is kind to us. This points out its power.

The Psalmist was wise to pray, "Set a guard over my mouth, O LORD; keep watch over the door of my lips" (Ps. 141:3). He knew the power of the tongue for the destruction of another person's self-esteem. James knew it, too. He wrote, "The tongue also is a fire, a world of evil among the parts of the body. It corrupts the whole person, sets the whole course of his life on fire, and is itself set on fire by hell. All kinds of animals, birds, reptiles and creatures of the sea are being tamed and have been tamed by man, but no man can tame the tongue. It is a restless evil, full of deadly poison" (Jas. 3:6-8). The one who can allow kindness, as a fruit of the Spirit, to control his restless tongue is an achiever. "He who loves a pure heart and whose speech is gracious will have the king for his friend" (Prov. 22:11).

Ralph Waldo Emerson wrote, "You can never do a kindness too soon, for you never know how soon it will be too late." How true this is! Everyone has memories, still painful perhaps, of words or acts we put off doing or saying to someone until it was too late. I have conducted many funeral services and have run across several families who tried to assuage their guilt of neglecting "grandma" by spending hundreds of dollars on flowers. Nothing against florists, but please: DO NOT WAIT! DO IT NOW! BE KIND TO THOSE YOU LOVE! LIVE THIS DAY AS IF IT WERE YOUR LAST! If this were your last day you would probably fall all over yourself in being gracious and loving to your family. Well, it might be. But even if it is not, treat others as the Lord has treated you.

The Bible is full of narratives of people who treated others kindly. Consider these examples. Young Joseph had been sold as a slave by his jealous brothers, but the plot did not end as they had predicted.

Joseph ended up by being, not a lowly servant, but a highly-placed officer in Egypt. His brothers fell on hard times so they went to Egypt in search of food. When they realized that Joseph was still alive they asked, "What if Joseph holds a grudge against us and pays us back for all the wrongs we did to him?" But Joseph answered, " 'Don't be afraid. Am I in the place of God? You intended to harm me, but God intended it for good to accomplish what is now being done, the saving of many lives. So then, don't be afraid. I will provide for you and your children.' And he reassured them and spoke kindly to them" (Gen. 50:15,19-21).

Godly midwives assisted in the birth of the Hebrew slaves in Egypt. The king of Egypt had ordered that if the newborn child were a male, the midwives were to kill it. If it were a female, they could let it live. The midwives refused to follow these instructions. "The midwives, however, feared God and did not do what the king of Egypt had told them to do; they let the boys live. Then the king of Egypt summoned the midwives and asked them, 'Why have you done this? Why have you let the boys live?' The midwives answered Pharaoh, 'Hebrew women are not like Egyptian women; they are vigorous and give birth before the midwives arrive.' " How were these women rewarded for this kindness? "So God was kind to the midwives and the people increased and became even more numerous. And because the midwives feared God, he gave them families of their own" (Ex. 1:17-20).

A widow named Ruth and her mother-in-law Naomi journeyed back to Naomi's home in Bethlehem. They met a man named Boaz who allowed the two women to enter his fields and pick up whatever grain the other workers left behind. Boaz gave these orders to his men, "Even if she gathers among the sheaves, don't embarrass her. Rather, pull out some stalks for her from the bundles and leave them for her to pick up, and don't rebuke her" (Ruth 2:15-16). So Ruth gleaned in the field until late in the evening and went home with plenty to eat, and even some left over. Eventually Ruth and Boaz married and had a son who became the grandfather of David. Who knows where a simple kindness might lead?

When David was king of Israel he searched for someone of Saul's family to whom he could show gratitude. A man named Mephibosheth, the son of Jonathan who had been David's close friend, was found. He was summoned before David. " 'Don't be afraid,' David said to him, 'for I will surely show you kindness for the sake of your father Jonathan. I will restore to you all the land that belonged to your grandfather Saul, and you will always eat at my table' " (2 Sam. 9:7). Some debts are longstanding but come due with much interest accrued.

Paul, on one of his many voyages, was in a shipwreck. When he reached the shore he found a pleasant surprise for himself and the others. "Once safely on shore, we found out that the island was called Malta. The islanders showed us unusual kindness. They built a fire and welcomed us all because it was raining and cold" (Acts 28:1-2). Here was simple human compassion.

Jesus once told a story about a man in whom the milk of human kindness had not soured. The man, himself the victim of discrimination and irrational hatred, traveled along a narrow road and found another victim. This victim, however, had been the target of muggers who had left him for dead. The fellow traveling the road waited for nothing but picked up the injured man, set him on his donkey, and carried him to an inn where he could be helped. This kind man has been immortalized in history and his very name symbolizes compassion—the good Samaritan (Luke 10:25-37). He had known hate and rejection because he was thought of as a "half breed." But he realized that hate had to seep into his heart to cause the most damage, and he refused to allow that. So one victim could feel compassion for another and act kindly toward him.

Learning the Kindness of Christ

A little girl had found a turtle in her yard but could not coax it out of its shell. Her uncle watched for a while as the girl tried everything she could. Finally he said, "If you put him by the fireplace, he'll warm up after while and come out by himself." Then, as almost an afterthought, the uncle added, "People are sorta' like terrapins. Never try to force a fellow into anything. Just warm him up with a little human kindness, and more'n likely he'll come your way."[2] This comes easier for some than others. Some people seem gifted with the ability to "warm up" others with kindness, while the rest of us have to struggle. We may not lack the desire to be kind but are short on technique. If so, that can be learned to some degree. Paul wrote to the Colossians to clothe themselves with kindness. This calls to mind an image of a person dressing himself. That being so, we can learn to "dress" ourselves with kindness.

When William Penn was given land in the New World by King Charles II, he was also granted power to make war on the Indians. But Penn refused to build forts or have soldiers in his province. Instead, he treated the Indians kindly and as equals. All disputes between the two races were settled by a meeting of six white men and six Indians. When Penn died the Indians mourned him as a friend. After Penn's death, other colonies were constantly under attack by the Indians. Pennsylvania was free from such attacks, however, as long as they refused to arm themselves. Many years later the Quakers were outvoted in the State, and the colony began building forts and training soldiers against possible aggression. You can guess what happened. They were immediately attacked.

Learning the ethic of the second mile has its roots in childhood, of course. A child who grows up with careful guidance on relating to others has a jump on one who learns to treat others as enemies or mere nuisances. Parents need to give their children guidance in both why and how to treat others with respect. This calls for taking time with the kids. My twin boys recently "graduated" from nursery school. They marched up to the front when their names were called and proudly received their "diplomas." Carla and I had taken the day off and promised the boys we would go to their favorite restaurant and then see a movie. It was a disaster! They wouldn't eat the hamburgers after begging for them; we couldn't find a suitable movie, so they howled like little banshees. Then they missed their afternoon nap and were crabby all evening. It didn't matter, though, because I wouldn't have missed that day for the world. Sharing that day, howls and all, was fun.

Some children don't do well in nursery schools, but my guys have thrived. They have learned as much as the average kindergarten child regarding the ABCs, but they also learned something more important. Their teachers have shown all the children how to share toys and to treat each other with kindness and care. Kindness is not some "magical" virtue which falls fully-grown from heaven. It must be learned—if not as a child, then as an adult. Sometimes it is the art of seeing life through another's eyes and acting on the insight.

Kindness is doing what you can to help others, even when it seems unconventional and unique. One lady did this in an unusual manner. She volunteered to work in a children's hospital. Several times each week this lady dresses as a clown and goes around the wards playing with the children. Even though she would rather avoid it if possible, there are times when she encounters children who are crying with pain. She carries popcorn with her. When she finds a child crying she takes a kernel of popcorn and touches it to his/her cheek to absorb the tears. Then she offers it to the child, or she pops it into her mouth. Then the two of them sit for a while and eat tears. For some reason, it really helps the children.[3] Eating tears! Sharing pain. Who but the kind would do that?

Ezekiel did somewhat the same as he sat with the exiles in Tel Aviv. He wrote, "I came to the exiles who lived at Tel Aviv near the Kebar River. And there, where they were living, I sat among them for seven days—overwhelmed" (Ezek. 2:15).

Think about your experiences. Who has helped you the most, one who stood aloof from you and preached pious sermonettes, or one who became involved in your struggles and "ate tears" with you? There certainly is a place for sermons, but not if they are somehow divorced from the twentieth century and individual lives.

Kindness is the willingness to throw in with others for a shared life. I do not mean that everyone should run out and join a commune. What I am suggesting is that we begin to see ourselves as part of a great community—the church. The early Christians related to this, but American Christianity is so individualistic that we have a difficult time understanding. To be kind, in the biblical sense, is to see yourself as partially responsible both to and for others, and to act accordingly.

Not long ago I drove onto a parking lot in New Orleans and had my attention drawn to an old Chevy. Across the trunk the owner had put in large black letters: AVENGE YOURSELF—LIVE LONG

ENOUGH TO BE A PROBLEM TO YOUR CHILDREN. I had a laugh out of that portable advertisement for revenge, but it also reminded me of situations that are not funny. Far too many people carry grudges, resentments, and even deep hatreds throughout their lives. Talk of living out the biblical meaning of kindness is empty where anger and hatred are the motivating forces in a person's life. To learn kindness is to learn to forgive others. Otherwise life will be stunted and deformed.

Composer Frederick Chopin once visited the home of a friend and watched the family dog chase its tail around and around. Chopin later wrote a piece of music to accompany tail-chasing. He called it "The Little Dog Waltz," now known today as "The Minute Waltz." I have on occasion thought "The Little Dog Waltz" was the theme song for my life. At times I seem to be spinning in circles—virtually chasing my own tail. When I halt the vertigo long to examine what is wrong I usually find that my equilibrium is upset by attitudes of anger or resentment. These are such boomerang emotions. I throw them at someone else, but they always seem to come back to the thrower. They hurt me far more than others. I once heard that, "Anger is a craving for salt from someone who is dying of thirst." If we would learn to be kind, as the Bible instructs us, we will first have to cleanse ourselves of the negative attitudes and emotions which prohibit kindness.

Survey most of the TV situation comedies which are on now. Most of them use put-down humor to get laughs. Put-down humor is one person insulting or degrading another. This is the simplest form of humor for TV writers to come up with, but it is also the most destructive. This style of humor strips others of their self-respect and proper love for themselves. (Remember, Jesus did say to love your neighbor *as you love yourself.*) The constant insulting that goes on in television under the name of humor is a destructive force. It carries over into real life. Children and adults alike learn to think that they are sophisticated by being cynical and sarcastic toward others, but can you really believe this is the best way to live and treat others? A reporter interviewed Bill Cosby about the phenomenal success of his show. The reporter wanted to know why *The Cosby Show* was so successful. Cosby replied that people are hungry to see programs where a husband and wife love each other and show it. People crave to participate in a drama where children are treated with loving respect and taught strong moral values. This is what Cosby's show tries to do.

One of the kindest things parents can do is to make time for their children. I often observe the lack of kindness toward children (and also fail sometimes in this area). Too often we adults tend to assume the world of a child is trivial and unimportant. Maybe we could learn from the lady who walked along a path in a city park with her daughter. As they passed the park fountain the little girl saw the spray diffuse the sunlight into rainbows. She called this to her mother's attention. The mother told the girl to hurry before they missed their bus. But she saw the innocent joy of the face of the girl as she watched the rainbows, so this mother stopped, put her arms around the child, and they watched the rainbows together. She realized that another bus would come along, but they might never have another opportunity to watch rainbows in just this same way.[4]

My father is an old oilfield hand. This job meant that he was on twenty-four-hour call. He would often be gone from home for days at a time when trouble at the rig necessitated his being there. He was always busy, but in his crazy schedule I seldom felt cheated or deprived of time with him.

During the summers and holidays our family would often go to the rig location with him. We lived in Louisiana, and he often had to work in Texas, so we would rent some little low-cost house wherever he was. My older brother Glenn and I would go to the drilling site with Daddy. If the rig were near a body of water, we would fish. If we were near a marsh, we would duck hunt. We never went on a "vacation" in the usual sense. My father never had that kind of time or money, but he did know how to give attention to his children. One of the best Christmas dinners I ever had was at the rig. The rig was "stacked"— not operating—for the holidays, and he had to stay with it to prevent thefts. My mother, sister Linda, brother Glenn, and I stayed with Daddy in the bunk house for several days during the Christmas break at school. On Christmas day we ate Spam and crackers and drank Pepsi, and it was wonderful!

As I grew older I had wished to be in a family that was more "regular"—with the father working a "regular" job, coming home every night, and going off for vacations. Only later did I realize that we *were* regular. I had some mythical image in my mind about what a family should be and do. As I look back now, I realize Daddy always wanted to be home when he could and wanted us to be with him when we could. Many of my friends I considered "regular" never did half of what I did, never traveled half as much, and never felt the special love and kindness of a father as I did.

My wife, Carla, grew up in an even stranger setting. Her father was a salesman for a small company. He was considered self-employed but often was broke. They moved around all the time and never had any money to speak of, but her parents made life an adventure and fun. They gave themselves to Carla and her older sister Diane. That is the key. Children need the love and concern—which is what kindness is—of parents. The rest, such as a fancy house, big car, annual vacation, and so on, is fluff and unnecessary for real happiness.

Make the best of what you have now. Show your children rainbows. If you cannot have turkey and dressing then eat lunch meat and crackers, but do it with a sense of adventure, love, and kindness. If you cannot vacation at Yellowstone National Park, then keep your eyes open for the marvels of nature and places of historical interest in your own area. Most of us "ordinary" people miss so much of what we *can* see and do because we concentrate on what we *cannot* have. Concentrate on what you already have and can do. Be kind to yourself. You deserve it!

Glen Campbell used to sing a song which spoke of the need for kindness, "Try a Little Kindness." It is good advice for all of us, but for Christians it is more than that. It is an ethical imperative. Jesus taught an ethic of the second mile, doing more than is necessary, giving instead of only trying to get. People need what you have to offer, so "Try a Little Kindness."

6

For Goodness' Sake—
Goodness

*Goodness consists not in the outward things we do, but in the
inward thing we are. To be good is a great thing.*
— *Edwin Hubbell Chapin*

Hermits living in the desert may not be able to find much to quarrel about, but the rest of us are not so fortunate! Strife seems to be our middle name. Any two people being together seem to be like flint and steel to make sparks. Yet most people really do want to get along with others. The inability to get along with others has wreaked havoc on both personal and international levels. On the personal level, it has injured or even ended careers of people who seem promising. Dr. William Menninger has discovered remarkable statistics regarding people who have been fired from their jobs in industry. Social incompetence accounts for 60 percent to 80 percent of the failures. Only about 20 to 40 percent are due to technical incompetence.[1] Who can estimate the destruction caused on an international level because people have difficulty getting along? What would have happened if a young man named Adolf Hitler had been an easygoing, friendly fellow?

Paul taught that a fruit of the Spirit is goodness. This is not a false, self-conscious, and forced "goodness." Instead, Paul had in mind a quality close to generosity.[2] It is the ability to give, to give in, to reach out, and to care. It is the inner structure of moral life and ethical thought. We might think of a person's interior and emotional life as being like a bank account. If one is "in the black," with assets in reserve, he can be generous and loving. But if one's inner account is "in the red" and running a deficit, there will be nothing left to give. A friend of mine is having deep-seated emotional problems at the time of this writing. His emotional life is "in the red" to a large extent. A trained counselor is working with my friend to help him regain his sense of emotional balance. If this fails, my friend might never be able to express the fruit of the Spirit of God which is called goodness. How can someone who is emotionally bankrupt be good in the sense of being generous in his attitudes and actions toward others?

Finding Inner Goodness

Paul was not thinking of a person who is "goody-goody." No one likes such a person. I have a friend who says he has a good "BD"— "Baloney Detector." He has the ability to sniff out insincerity in someone at one hundred yards. He can tell when someone is putting on a front and when that person is being genuine. Actually, the church would be better off if everyone had a good "BD." [Theological seminaries used to give BD's—Bachelor of Divinity degrees, but that is another story.]

Of course, not everyone even likes genuine goodness. Do you remember the old television program, *All in the Family?* The central characters were Archie and Edith Bunker. One evening the two of them had the following conversation:

Archie: That's you all right, Edith the Good. You'll stoop to anything to be good. You never yell. You never swear. You never make nobody mad. You think it's easy living with a saint? Even when you cheat, you don't cheat to win. You cheat to lose. Edit', you ain't human.

Edith: That's a terrible thing to say, Archie Bunker. I am just as human as you are.

Archie: Oh yeah . . . then prove you're just as human as me. Do something rotten.[3]

Poor Edith's dilemma is similar to many people, some of whom are reading this book. Perhaps you live around people, perhaps close family—husbands or wives—who do not have the same outlook on life as you. You feel the dialogue between Archie and Edith as a stinging reminder that, even when you try doing your best and being all you can be, some people misunderstand. They mock or jeer or, maybe even worse, hold your ideals to scorn. Appropriating the fruit of the Spirit known as goodness is no simple task. It never has been.

The best man who ever lived was motivated by His inner love, generosity, and concern for man as well as by His devotion to his Heavenly Father. But those inner ideals were not enough to keep our spiritual ancestors from spiking the Lord Jesus to a cross.

It is a mystery that people who value excellence on the football field seem to care nothing about excellence on the moral gridiron. During a recent Super Bowl, an estimated 85 million people watched two teams who were supposed to be the best. Kicking, running, passing, blocking, and other moves were executed to their highest level possible. Why would not these same 85 million people tune in to watch a special program about men, women, and children who have demonstrated a spirit of excellence in the moral and ethical aspects of life? There are many answers to this question, of course, but one of them has to do with the aversion people have toward genuinely good people. Why does Archie resent Edith's goodness? Why do the spouses of some of you reading this book resent your generous approach to others? Part of the reason is that your attitude threatens them, and no one likes to feel threatened.

Paul wrote to his friend Titus about the grace of God: "It teaches us to say 'No' to ungodliness and worldly passions, and to live self-controlled, upright and godly lives in this present age, while we wait for the blessed hope—the glorious appearing of our great God and Savior, Jesus Christ, who gave himself for us to redeem us from all wickedness and to purify for himself a people that are his very own, *eager to do what is good*" (Titus 2:12-14, italics added). To live in Christ is to live in the desire and the ability for goodness in its deepest meaning—goodness as part of who I am and not just merely I do.

We find inner goodness through the inner transformation which occurs in our relationship with Christ. This is a *lifelong* process which is never complete. It is a goal toward which to move, but one which in this life is never fully reached. This need not cause despair. I simply realize that I will never attain complete inner goodness on this planet. I am too flawed, too hemmed in my by own weaknesses and problems. My hope is that I look to Christ who is "the author and perfecter of our faith" (Heb. 12:2). In order to find genuine inner goodness, we must avoid a false variety.

Avoiding Short-Sighted "Goodness"

People have the right to be repulsed by people who mistake their own prudish or short-sighted views for the voice of the Almighty. In 1800 a small pamphlet entitled, "Excerpt From the Memoirs of Caroline E. Smelt," was published. Miss Smelt, it seems, was an insufferable prude who thought of herself as the paragon of virtue. On her deathbed she sent the following message to her cousin: "Tell her never to enter a theatre, never to play cards, never to attend tea parties. For if any one of these is evil, they all are; and of this I am absolutely certain."[4] The world is full of the likes of Caroline E. Smelt—always ready to pass judgment on everyone and every activity based on her, or his, own limited view of life. The Scriptures promise that the Christian is free in Christ, and that Jesus gives an abundant life (John 10:10). He paid a high price for me, and I refuse to allow the Caroline Smelts of this world—however well-meaning they might appear—to squeeze my mind into their purses or briefcases. No wonder Henry David Thoreau once wrote, "If I knew . . . that a man was coming to my house with the conscious design of doing me good, I should run for my life."

Freedom in Christ gives freedom *for good* as well as freedom *from evil.* Paul wrote about the confidence which comes from a relationship with Christ: "Such confidence as this is ours through Christ before God. Not that we are competent in ourselves to claim anything for ourselves, but our competence comes from God. He had made us competent as ministers of a new covenant—not of the letter but of the Spirit; *for the letter kills, but the Spirit gives life.*" (2 Cor. 3:4-6, italics added)

Every generation has its own form of Pharisaism—an attitude which sets itself up as judge and jury of every issue. For example, you can turn on television all through the week and hear a variety of preachers speaking about every issue imaginable. The medium of television is powerful and makes many of these ministers seem more knowledgeable than they really are. As one person commented to me, "If these people are on television, they *must* know what they're talking about." Perhaps—but perhaps not. Any time a person uses his pulpit to tell others, in no uncertain terms, what to think about every matter under heaven and how to act, that is an illegitimate use of power. God gave each of us brains and expects us to utilize them.

My purpose here is simply to point out that what "Brother" or "Sister Soandso" thinks is good for them, may not be good for you. Good, in an absolute sense, is unchangeable, but the good you and I seek and find may be relative. Take the matter of table prayer before meals. My family and I pray before meals and enjoy it. But that does not mean anyone who does not pray before meals is a "sinner."

Take one further example. Outward forms of religion do not necessarily indicate inner goodness, nor does inner goodness always express itself in particular outward ways. An old Baptist preacher was once conducting a revival in the backwoods near the Sabine River many years ago. In the midst of his sermon, while exhorting the sinners to flee from the wrath to come, the following incident happened.

> A tall, stove-hatted, high-collared, Prince-Alberted, double-breasted, vandyked-whiskered man carrying a gold-headed cane, came walking down the aisle and seated himself near the front. The preacher glanced at Him, but kept on exhorting. He had several mourners "well worked up at the moment." But unable to resist attention to the distinguished stranger, he finally turned to him and said: "My friend, are you a Christian?" The distinguished gentleman replied: "Sir, I am a theological professor." "My Lord," said the preacher, "I wouldn't let a little thing like that keep me from coming to Christ. . . . You can't be saved with anything between you and God."[5]

We have a difficult time coming to grips with our lack of goodness. We might group ourselves together with people who look just like us, talk just like us, dress just like us, and even act just like us. This grouping, whether it is a club or a church, often has the function of keeping out other attitudes of looking at life. In some cases this is helpful and necessary. But in other instances this "fortress" mentality is harmful.

I take seriously the declarations of the Bible about evil. Because of this, I am always suspicious of people who act and talk as if they themselves have no taint of troubles, problems, or sin. Certainly I *want* people to develop and display goodness as a fruit of the Spirit of God. But what I do not want to see is people merely fooling themselves into believing that they have somehow overcome all temptation and that they always act from only the purest motives. The irony of all this is that the one who thinks he is good, probably is not.

What I am saying here is touchy, so let me recap for a moment. The Bible tells us that one fruit of the Spirit of God is goodness. Goodness is a quality of life which begins on the inside and moves to the outside. It is marked with a high sense of self-awareness and truthfulness. A genuinely good person does not go around all the time playing "Little Jack Horner"—"see what a good boy am I." Goodness is open to growth and correction precisely because it realizes it has not yet arrived. Goodness in humans which pretends to perfection is false and dangerous. As the Scriptures put it, "Pride goes before destruction, a haughty spirit before a fall" (Prov. 16:18). Goodness is never satisfied with itself nor proud of its achievements, but is forever on the lookout for new growth, new understanding, new ways to change more into the image of the Master. Above all, it is not false or put-on.

A "good" man or woman, in the biblical sense, always seeks to model his or her life after Jesus who "went around doing good." (Acts 10:38) But he does not make excuses for his failures nor does he blame them on others. The good man does not injure others through words or deeds and then try to protect himself by saying, "Well, God told me to say this" or "The Lord made me do this." A few years ago a television comedian used to get laughs by doing something outrageous and then alibiing, "The devil made me do it." That is an unacceptable explanation. This tendency to offer excuses was noticed by a psychologist who works closely with people who seek his help. He wrote:

> On our pilgrimage, we are defeated not only by the narrowness of
> our perspective, and our fear of the darkness, but by our excuses as
> well. How often we make circumstances our prison, and other people
> our jailers. If only I were not married or if at least my wife were not
> so cautious, what great ventures I could pursue. Translation: It's a good
> thing my wife takes responsibility for reminding me of the hazards of
> some undertakings; . . . In this way I can act with realistic caution,

while maintaining the image of myself as the undaunted adventurer. . . .

At my best, I take full responsibility for what I do and for what I choose not to do. I see that there is no prison except that which I construct to protect myself from feeling my pain, from risking my losses.[6]

The name Jim Jones conjures up memories of the People's Temple where over 900 people committed suicide in the name of their religious beliefs. They felt that God wanted them dead rather than alive, but people under the influence of a dictator like Jones do not think clearly. This brings us to a most important matter: How do we know what God wants? This book is not about God's will, but I do want to write about it as related to goodness.

One way to find out what God wants is to realize what He forbids. The Ten Commandments offer good guidance here. Next, search the Scriptures to find those major sections which offer guidance on what God requires. The Sermon on the Mount in Matthew 5 through 7 is helpful here. Further, look at the New Testament teaching on spiritual gifts. Christians are given specific gifts by the Spirit. Part of knowing what God's will is for our lives is to consider these gifts and to learn which one(s) are present. Then the task is to cultivate them and put them into practice.[7] Beyond this, let me communicate something very vital about our knowledge of God:

PUT THIS IN BOLD LETTERS AND REMIND YOURSELF OF IT DAILY: GOD IS BIGGER THAN ANY OF OUR IDEAS ABOUT HIM. HE CALLS US TO A LIFE OF COURAGEOUS AND STRAIGHTFORWARD ACTION. TO BE CHRISTIAN IS NOT TO RETREAT FROM LIFE AND HIDE FROM ITS PAINS. IT IS, INSTEAD, TO LIVE IN THE FREEDOM FOR GOOD THINGS.

The Courage to be Good

We need moral and intellectual courage to cultivate the fruit of the Spirit known as goodness. To be a coward and hide from life requires no courage and little effort. The trouble with that is that you end up at the finish of your life with nothing to show for your days. I do not want to spend my life hiding from imaged pain. I do not want to waste my energy, which is renewable but still limited, watching television all the time when I could talk to neighbors, write letters to friends, play games with my children, or expand my mind with a good book. More than this, though, I do not want to dodge my responsibility as a community person by refusing to work in my community for its betterment. Goodness is a virtue which leads us to become involved with people and their troubles, as well as their triumphs.

One of the reasons why the church does not do better in winning people to Christ is that many folks see Christians as basically selfish. Those outside the church sometimes think of Christians as weaklings who have "feathered their nests" with the belief they are special to "their God," as it is sometimes put. They note the absence of Christians in certain areas of life such as politics and peacemaking ventures, and wonder why, if Christ makes people stronger and better, these Christians are not more involved in life. After all, don't these Christians tell of a Christ who refused to stay in a privileged place in heaven but chose to come live in the rough-and-tumble world of people?

Herman Melville, best known as the author of *Moby Dick,* once wrote of a commodore on a man-of-war ship:

> It beseemed him . . . to erect himself into an example of virtue, and show the gun-deck what virtue was. But alas! when Virtue sits high aloft on a frigate's poop, when Virtue is crowned in the cabin a commodore, when Virtue rules by compulsion, and domineers over Vice as a slave, then Virtue, though her mandates be outwardly observed, bears little interior sway. To be efficacious, Virtue must come down from aloft, even as our blessed Redeemer came down to redeem our whole man-of-war world; to that end, mixing with its sailors and sinners as equals.[8]

When our "goodness" sees itself as the paragon of virtue and goes out to prove itself good, it usually ends up doing the opposite. When this "goodness" heads out on a witch hunt it often bags the wrong quarry.[9] I know of a fellow who once knelt on a busy sidewalk to pray for the salvation of all the "sinners" around him. He blocked the flow of people on the sidewalk so a policeman politely touched him on the shoulder with his billyclub and asked him to move. The man on his knees spat out viciously, "Man, if you touch me again, I'll pray that God will wither up your hand!" So much for a loving witness!

Recently 1,534 people were asked to rank on a scale of 1 to 7 their beliefs about human nature. On this scale, 1 represented "basically good" and each successive number representing less good. The number 7 represented "perverse and corrupt." The results were these: 27.2 percent ranked human nature with a 1—basically good; 20.6 percent ranked it a 2; 17.5 percent gave it a 3; 17.2 percent ranked human nature with a 4 which represents "equally good and perverse;" 5.6 percent ranked it with a 5; 3.0 percent gave it a 6; and 6.8 percent ranked human nature with a 7—"perverse and corrupt."[10] This poll proves nothing other than the fact that many people feel human nature is basically good and that people simply need the right kind of opportunities to demonstrate goodness.

But the biblical teaching on this matter is otherwise. You cannot read the New Testament without coming to the conclusion that much is fundamentally wrong with people. The Bible calls our condition "sin." Some people suggest: all that is wrong with people is that they live in a bad environment, or that their subconscious mind is making them behave badly, or that they simply have not learned how to act correctly.

All of these factors do affect behavior, of course. But are they the major factors in our sinful human nature? The Scriptures declare that a person must be born again, must repent of his sins, must be remade from God. This is not a view of human nature which suggests that it is only slightly flawed, but rather that something is dramatically and tragically defective. I take this view seriously. To appropriate the biblical meaning of goodness, then, requires an inner transformation of a person. (If you have never had this happen, I urge you to talk with a person you know is a serious Christian. One of these people can tell you how to experience this inner transformation. The New Testament calls this change salvation. It is not only for a select few, but for any who wish to be related to God through faith.)

This is not much different from some fine people I know who attend church regularly and seem to be fully involved in the life of faith. But the children of some of these people have announced that they felt "called" to ministry, and their parents nearly went berserk. "You're going to waste your life" or "Son, there ain't no money in preaching" or "Dear, you have such a fine future in accounting. Why ruin it with this missionary stuff?" Do not think I am exaggerating here. I have seen this happen several times. This is a lesson about the life of faith, too. Someone is always willing to control your life if you do not. While I favor talking about ideas and plans with family and friends, this should not be an excuse for failing to live up to the goodness of which we are capable.

All of this requires great courage. We might as well face the fact that we cannot be good without being courageous. Goodness is both inner moral strength and outward ethical action. No wonder the New Testament declares that God gives this through his Spirit. This is nothing that can be manufactured on demand. A doctor thought about this matter of courage, especially among some of his patients, and wrote:

> Life is beautiful, but it is hard for all human beings, very hard even for the majority. It is even harder in misfortune, in the face of depriva- tion. That requires a lot of courage. I stress that fact because I am well aware that it is something of which I have very little. My own courage revives when I come into contact with courageous people—often my patients, more handicapped than I am, and displaying courage which I admire. For courage is not taught, it is caught. Society is a vast laboratory of mutual encouragement. Each member can give the other only the courage he has himself—doctors as well as patients.[16]

God grant that we might acquire the courage to be good. God grant, too, that we rub elbows with genuinely good people, for good- ness, like courage, is not taught—but caught.

7

Held in Firm Grip— Faithfulness

Without faithfulness, we are like stained glass windows in the dark.—Anonymous

Paul gave us a clue when he spoke of part of the fruit of the Spirit as "faithfulness." You and I can reach the end of life with bedrock, quiet confidence by being faithful to our Lord, to our families, and especially to ourselves.

This word in the original language is *pistis* and is translated as "faith" in some older versions of the Bible. But most newer versions translate it in Galatians 5:22 as "faithfulness." The reason is explained clearly by William Barclay. He noted that *faith* means

> absolute trust, absolute self-surrender, absolute confidence, absolute obedience in regard to Jesus Christ. This is what might be called a theological virtue; it is rather the basis of belief and the basis of our whole relationship to God through Jesus Christ. But the virtues listed in the fruit of the Spirit are not *theological* virtues; they are *ethical* virtues: they have to do not so much with our relationship to God as with our relationship to our fellow-men. What *pistis* here means is not *faith* but *faithfulness;* it it the quality of reliability, trustworthiness, which makes a man a person on whom we can utterly rely and whose word we can utterly accept.[1]

Barclay's explanation helps us understand what Paul is trying to communicate. This trustworthiness and reliability is an inner strength and quality of one who yields his life to the Spirit of God. The man or woman with the quality of faithfulness can be counted on and trusted.

Jesus spoke of those who tried artificial or external means of insuring the truthfulness of their word by swearing oaths. Jesus' prohibition against oaths points out that no external binder can make a dishonest person honest. Jesus said, "Again, you have heard that it was said to the people long ago, 'Do not break your oath, but keep the oaths you have made to the Lord.' But I tell you, Do not swear at all: either by heaven, for it is God's throne; or by the earth, for it is his footstool; or by Jerusalem, for it is the city of the Great King. And do not swear by your head, for you cannot make even one hair white or black. Simply let your 'Yes' be 'Yes,' and your 'No,' 'No'; anything beyond this comes from the evil one" (Matt. 5:33-37).

I once knew a man who was a notorious liar. No one believed anything he said because he seemed to prefer a lie to the truth. Whenever he would try to convince someone of his honesty, he would add the kicker, "I swear on my Mother's grave." I often think of this fellow when I remember Jesus' words about letting my yes be yes and my no be no. Jesus wants his followers to be true to their word. If my inner life—my thinking and my emotions—are so fouled up that I cannot distinguish the truth from a lie, then I cannot properly bear this fruit of the Spirit. If I am in turmoil on the inside, then my actions will probably betray my condition. What we need, then, is a means of ordering our inner lives so they are under control. We need faithfulness.

The Faithfulness of God

Christians reflect faithfulness because their Lord is faithful. The Bible is a witness to a faithful God who does what He says He will do. Here are some of the things which God is faithful in doing.

God is faithful in establishing and keeping his covenants (agreements) with his people. Moses told the people who had come out of the Egyptian slavery: "Know therefore that the LORD your God is God; he is the faithful God, keeping his covenant of love to a thousand generations of those who love him and keep his commands" (Deut. 7:9). The writer of the Book of Hebrews notes a similar promise. Referring to the Lord's promise to give salvation to those how trust Him, the writer says, "Let us hold unswervingly to the hope we profess, for he who promised is faithful" (Heb. 10:23).

God is faithful in calling people to Himself. Paul said, "God, who has called you into fellowship with his Son Jesus Christ our Lord, is faithful" (1 Cor. 1:9). The psalmist declared, "I will sing of the love of the LORD forever; with my mouth I will make your faithfulness known through all generations" (Ps. 89:1).

God is faithful in not allowing us to be crushed by the burdens we bear. Paul wrote, "No temptation has seized you except what is common to man. And God is faithful; he will not let you be tempted beyond what you can bear. But when you are tempted, he will also provide a way out so that you can stand up under it" (1 Cor. 10:13).

God is faithful in helping His people mature thoroughly. Paul wrote, "May God himself, the God of peace, sanctify you through and through. May your whole spirit, soul and body be kept blameless at the coming of our Lord Jesus Christ. The one who calls you is faithful and he will do it" (1 Thess. 5:23-4).

God is faithful in protecting His people from evil. "But the Lord is faithful, and he will strengthen and protect you from the evil one. We have confidence in the Lord that you are doing and will continue to do the things we command. May the Lord direct your hearts into God's love and Christ's perseverance" (2 Thess. 3:3-4).

God is faithful to His own truth. Paul asked, "What if some did not have faith? Will their lack of faith nullify God's faithfulness? Not at all! Let God be true, and every man a liar" (Rom. 3:3-4*a*). In writing to Timothy Paul declared, "If we are faithless, he will remain faithful, for he cannot disown himself" (2 Tim. 2:13).

To all of this William Barclay noted, "With one voice the (biblical) writers witness to that which they themselves had over and over again experienced—the great truth that we can depend on God."[2] If God is faithful, trustworthy, and capable of being believed, it follows that those who claim to love Him likewise be faithful. When a person commits his life to God through Christ, that commitment is something like a marriage vow. In fact, it is even better because it nowhere states, "Till death do us part." A commitment in faith says something like this: "Lord, I promise to give myself to You and to follow Your leading in faith. I vow to be faithful to this calling every day of my life. Where I am weak, give me strength. Where I am ignorant, give me knowledge. Where I am arrogant, give me humility. Where I am disquieted, give me patience. Father, I give myself to You through your Son."

This is not easy to do, and I would not want to suggest otherwise. To commit your life to God is a decision which changes your outlook, your perspective, your will, and your actions. You wind up in that strange tension between knowing God but at the same time always seeking to know Him more. Even when times are tough, the knowledge of the trustworthiness of God carries us through. A Russian Baptist who is in a labor camp because of his faith, expressed this fact in the following prayer/poem:

> Behind the bars of a murky prison
> Days and nights with prayer I
>   meet.
> And in the presence of resentment
>   and evil I feel the prayers of my
>   friends.
>
> God gives me quiet sleep,
> Though the restless people don't
>   sleep.
> And although the hours to me are
>   unknown,
> During the night he awakens me
>   twice,
>
> So that I'd hear him in the quiet,
> At three or four every night.
> Someone, somewhere from his
>   whole heart
> For me before God is interceding.
>
> And tears run down my cheeks,
> And to God ascends a grateful
>   prayer.
> I'm in prison often interrogated;
> Though the prayers of friends I'm
>   strengthened.
>
> Do not carelessly waste your days,

My dear friends, for you know
　　yourselves
In bonds, strength and power are
　　seen,
For a prison is a real exam.[3]

How strange it seems, at least on the surface, that in conditions almost unimaginably bad, this Christian knows of the faithfulness of God. And this is true not just of people in prison camps in Russia, but true of people everywhere who turn to Him for support.

Flannery O'Connor, the late novelist from Georgia, was a devout Christian who never faltered in her faith, even though she had an incurable illness and died at a fairly early age. She once wrote to one of her readers giving advice which I have found full of wisdom:

> What people don't realize is how much religion costs. They think faith is a big electric blanket, when of course, it is the cross. It is much harder to believe than not to believe, you must at least do this: keep an open mind. Keep it open toward faith, keep wanting it, keep asking for it, and leave the rest to God.[4]

Staying Faithful to Oneself

God is faithful to do as He promised he would. I do not doubt His veracity at all. My problem, and probably yours too, comes with my own faithfulness. Like most Christians, I have deep-seated beliefs about certain matters. These beliefs include the nature of God, the work of the church, and other theological matters. They also include ideas about how I should act.

Here is where I often fail because I am not consistent in my actions. I am not always loving toward people who dislike me, even though I believe I should be. I am not always generous toward people who try to use me for their own purposes, even though I feel I should try to work with them. (But this does not include allowing people to manipulate me.) I am not even always kind to my own family, even though they are the most important people in the world to me.

The saints of all ages have known the tension which exists for followers of Christ. They feel led of God in one direction but feel pulled by many forces in another direction. I know of no better statement of this dilemma than the one from Paul in Romans 7.

> We know that the law is spiritual; but I am unspiritual, sold as a slave to sin. I do not understand what I do. For what I want to do I do not do, but what I hate I do. And if I do what I do not what to do, I agree that the law is good. As it is, it is no longer I myself who do it, but it is sin living in me. I know that nothing good lives in me, that is, in my sinful nature. For I have the desire to do what is good, but I cannot carry it out. For what I do is not the good I want to do; no, the evil I do not want to do—this I keep on doing (Rom. 7:14-19).

After making this statement Paul says, "What a wretched man I am! Who shall rescue me from this body of death? Thanks be to God—through Jesus Christ our Lord!" (Rom. 7:24-5).

Most people with any sense of self-awareness can identify with Paul's situation. He confessed he had a sinful nature, and it was that nature which contributed to his dilemma. This is true for you and me, too. But for a short time, allow me to set aside a consideration of the nature of sin and plunge into the matter of faithfulness related to ourselves.

I have a hunch about why Christian people sometimes fail to live up to their potential. See if this makes sense to you. We often fail and blame the failure on sin, when in fact the failure is due simply to our not trying hard enough to avoid the behavior. Let me be specific. I sometimes lose my patience with my children. I raise my voice and sometimes speak harshly to them. When this happens I usually feel badly afterwards. I could shrug my shoulders and alibi, "Oh well, sin made me do this." But in fact nothing or nobody *made* me shout at my boys. I did it myself, and have nothing or no one to blame except myself. I must therefore work hard to "keep a lid on" myself and not go flying off the proverbial handle every time my children become a little loud.

This matter is true regarding much of what we value most. Building a life worthy of the Christian calling is tough, but worth all effort. A convicted murderer sat on "Death Row" in a Florida prison. He was a black man with seemingly very little going for him, but he found the forgiveness of God through his faith in Christ. He kept a journal of his days waiting for execution, and one entry reads as follows:

> Monday, June 7, 7:05 PM
>
> I wonder, what success have my classmates found? I know of those who found their graves with: needle in arm, bottle in hand, childbirth, police bullet.
>
> America, America, in teeth of your brutality I have nonetheless been fond of living in this land. Yet I am merely "nigger," without history, a thing upon the auction block. I am tempted to hate you, but hatred is a sickness, my friend. Thus, before each of your hands pulls the switch, though terrified and powerless, I will echo, "I love you." Thus will I remain Doug.[5]

Doug found that by refusing to hate the "system" and the people in it he could be faithful to his inner conviction of love. *Refusing to hate* —that is the key! We say things like, "He makes me so angry!" but in fact no one can *make* you angry without your permission.

I am often distressed with the way people in churches often seem to get their feelings hurt. I know of folks who have dropped out of church because of some unintended or innocent remark made to them. Others stopped attending because they felt someone had slighted them. I sometimes want to ask if we are such emotional infants who can be offended or hurt so easily. If someone does not speak to you at church, he may not be trying to avoid you or hurt you. He might be feeling an enormous load of inner conflict that has nothing to do with you. We would do well to give others the benefit of our generosity in attitude. And think about this: suppose someone did intentionally offend you or say something unkind to or about you. Does it really matter? Can their attitude actually injure you? *It cannot if you refuse to let it.* Be faithful to your own inner convictions, and you will find that few perceived slights will bother you.[6]

The question naturally arises, "How can I be faithful to myself?" One way is through what Lewis Smedes calls "the power of promising."[7] He asserts that this is the only way to overcome the unpredictability of the future. "If forgiving is the only remedy for your painful past, promising is the only remedy for your uncertain future." Folk wisdom often claims we cannot do anything about the future, but the fact is that we can affect the future. By deciding now about certain matters, I can control how I will act in certain situations in the future. For example, when I was married, I promised Carla to be a faithful husband. There have been times during our marriage when I found other women trying to "come on" to me. I refused to become involved with them because of a promise I had made years earlier. Consider the following.

Somewhere, perhaps close to you, there is a woman who is the wife of an alcoholic. She wants to throw in the towel and is tempted when secular wisdom advises, "Don't stay in a rough relationship—bail out at the earliest convenience." She has a desire to call an end to the problems of such a marriage. But she remembers the vows she made many years earlier—"for better or worse, in sickness and in health." These are her true convictions so she does the best she can for herself and her children. She investigates organizations such as Al-Anon and Al-A-Teen which offer help to families of alcoholics. The power of her promise keeps her steady personally, even if might not change the drinking habits of her husband. She is being faithful to herself.

Somewhere, perhaps close to you, there is a man whose son is running wild. He is driving the father crazy, and the man is tempted to tell the boy to pack his bags and hit the road. But he remembers the vows he made years earlier at the infant dedication service in his church. He promised to raise the boy and do the very best by him, no matter what. So he decides to do what he can for the boy while he is still under the father's roof. He is being faithful to himself.

Somewhere, perhaps close to you, there is a minister who has a first-class case of burnout. He is tired of encouraging other people who seem so ungrateful. He is sick to death of having to grind out two sermons or three each week for people who seem to care nothing for what he has to say. He is angry that the church has kept his salary frozen for three straight years, even though his education is comparable to the other executives and educators in the church. This minister wants to chuck the whole deal and go into some profession where he could make a decent living and feel that he contributes something to someone. But he thinks about his inner feeling of being called of God to be a minister. He remembers the vows he made years ago at his ordination service to serve wherever God calls him. So he renews his vows and takes a fresh look at the place of service he has now and goes on doing the best he can. He is being faithful to himself.

Three people—typical people really—who represent millions who have a tough time with certain situations in their lives. What keeps them going? Why should a woman stay with an alcoholic husband, even though their relationship could have been the basis of Thomas Hardy's description of a marriage as "stale familiarity"? And the father of the unruly son? Why not boot him out with the other million or so teenagers who run away from home or who are kicked out each year? Shouldn't he have to lie in the bed he made?

And what of the minister who feels so tired and disgusted? Why shouldn't he seek some place else to go where there might be a little more money, or opportunity, or realization of his worth on the part of the people?

The "why not" of all these questions is answered with one word—faithfulness. The apostle Paul knew more about hardship than most of us ever will, so he was certainly entitled to speak about it. He wrote to his young friend Timothy, "You then, my son, be strong in the grace that is in Christ Jesus. And the things you have heard me say in the presence of many witnesses entrust to reliable men who will also be qualified to teach others. Endure hardship with us like a good soldier of Christ Jesus" (2 Tim. 2:1-3). Endure. This is an ominous-sounding word, but without it faithfulness is impossible. This is true of any great undertaking. Edward Gibbon spent twenty years working on his monumental book, *The Decline and Fall of the Roman Empire.* Noah Webster worked for thirty-six years on the dictionary which bears his name. George Bancroft sifted notes and researched for twenty-six years to produce his classic work, *History of the United States.* The message is clear. If you want to produce anything worthwhile, especially a life, then remain faithful to your inner convictions. Someone said in relation to faithfulness:

> One of the commonest mistakes and one of the costliest is thinking
> that success is due to some genius, some magic—something or other

which we do not possess. Success is generally due to holding on, and failure to letting go. You decide to learn a language, study music, take a course of reading, train yourself physically. Will it be success or failure? It depends upon how much pluck and perseverance the word "decide" contains. The decision that nothing can overrule, the grip that nothing can detach will bring success. Remember the Chinese proverb, "With time and patience, the mulberry leaf becomes satin."[8]

Anything significant which is attained comes through hard work, at least on the part of someone. Even the person who is given everything on the fabled "silver platter" must realize that someone had to work hard for that money. The person who wants success in his chosen field must be willing to put in the time and effort to succeed. I have friends who want to write books, but they are not willing to undertake the hard work of writing. Until they do, they will dream of the "easy" life of the writer and imagine fat royalty checks coming in. This is a dream sure enough![9]

I am speaking here about being faithful to yourself, and this includes working to fulfill your goals. But allow me to remind you that life is not just hard work. The word "career" comes from the French meaning "race course," and thus a career can be just a rat race. Being faithful to God, to others, and to yourself also includes well-rounded and balanced living. This means that life is more than constant work. Recreation is literally *re*-creation—of mind, body, and spirit.

Faithfulness is a fruit of the Spirit which is a steadying influence in shaky and uncertain times. As such, it is like a hand which holds us in firm grip both to strengthen and to calm. Paul wrote to Timothy that "The Lord knows those who are his" (2 Tim. 2:19). The faithfulness of His hand holds us in a firm grip, even as we struggle to live in Him. Not a bad trade-off, right?

8
A Powerful Weakness—
Gentleness

The great mind knows the power of gentleness.—Robert Browning

What does the word *gentleness* suggest to you? Does it bring to mind a picture of a Caspar Milquetoast or a Barney Fife? Does it make you think of a self-loathing person who will not look another person in the eye, and who sees himself as merely the doormat for others to walk on? All of these images, and others equally repugnant, seem associated with the word *gentleness*. These, however, have very little to do with the biblical meaning of gentleness.

In Galatians 5:22, where Paul listed the fruit of the Spirit, gentleness does not suggest spinelessness and spiritlessness and a lack of strength. Some older versions of the Bible use the word *meekness* here, but this is even more apt to misunderstanding than "gentleness." The original word is *prautes,* but there seems no one English word that will fully carry over its meaning. Whatever else it means, it does *not* suggest weakness or lack of courage. Gentleness is a power which seems at first glance like a weakness. But it is "the power through which by the help of the Spirit of God the strong and explosive might of the passions is harnessed in the service of men and of God."[1]

As part of the fruit of the Spirit, gentleness is a powerful weakness. It holds itself in subjection to reserve its energy to accomplish its goals. We might think of it like this. The difference between a river and a swamp has to do with the banks. A swamp has no clearly defined banks, and so it oozes out all over. But a river, such as the Mississippi, has definite banks which hold it in the channel. A river thus flows powerfully rather than oozing listlessly. Gentleness is more like a river than a swamp. Its energy and power are harnessed for specific purposes.

Even so, many contemporary people have trouble thinking of themselves in terms of gentleness. This seems to be a quality which is not desired or valued. In Bud Blake's comic strip, "Tiger," a little boy stands and watches a girl carry a football past him. When his teammates criticize him for not tackling her, the boy says, "I was afraid I'd hurt her." The last frame of the strip shows this little boy walking home with head down and shoulders slumped, saying, "I got thrown out of the game for unnecessary gentleness."[2]

Who cannot identify with his dilemma? The church preaches meekness—gentleness, humility, "softness," (take your pick of synonyms here)—but almost no one else values it. Sheldon Vanauken went to Oxford University for graduate study. At that time he was not a Christian but began investigating the faith. He also began writing to C. S. Lewis about the claims of faith. In one of his letters to Lewis, Vanauken confessed that of all the elements of faith, humility (or gentleness) seemed on the surface the most repugnant. He wrote:

> Indeed, there is nothing in Christianity which is so repugnant to me as humility—the bent knee. If I knew beyond hope or despair that Christianity were true, my fight for ever would have to be against the pride of "the spine may break but it never bends."[3]

I think I understand why this man was so repulsed by the idea of humility. It was because he had a popular—and mistaken—view of what the Bible means by humility or gentleness. To be gentle does not mean to be inactive or docile. When I lose myself in Christ I do not simply cease to exist, but rather I emerge having found myself in a new way. As Jesus taught, "Whoever finds his life will lose it, and whoever loses his life for my sake will find it." Vanauken, and many others like him, understood the first half of Jesus' statement but not the second. I find my life when I so intertwine my life with Christ that I am no longer myself alone. Whatever else this might be, it is not boring!

Understanding Gentleness

The Bible has a cluster of words which convey a meaning similar to "gentleness." These include words such as *lowliness, meekness, patience,* and *foreberance.* All of these words, along with *gentleness,* signify someone who is so strong that he need not prove his strength. For example, Jesus is described like this. He invited, "Take my yoke upon you and learn from me, for I am gentle and humble in heart, and you will find rest for your souls" (Matt. 11:29). But His gentleness was no weakness. No one but an incredibly strong person could have lived with the abuse and misunderstanding that Jesus suffered, not to mention the worst abuse—the cross. He voluntarily surrendered His status as sovereign Lord to become one with us, to walk where we walk, to identify with us, and to suffer for us (See Phil. 2:5-11.) He was much too concerned about the welfare of others to spend His time and energy defending himself all the time. He had other work to do.

When I was in the seventh grade, a group of us were playing baseball at recess. The largest and strongest boy in our class was Cecil. One of the smallest was Jerry. During the game Cecil was playing second base. On one play Jerry was trying to make it from first. As Jerry came flying into second, he slammed into Cecil and fell down. He jumped up, pushed Cecil, and yelled, "Hey, watch it, boy!" All of us on the field held our breath as we imagined what Cecil was about to do to Jerry. I could almost see him pound poor little Jerry into the dust. Instead, Cecil just smiled and said, "Yes sir," and walked back to his base to resume play. The rest of us boys talked about that for a long time. Cecil displayed on the baseball field an attitude which was close to what the New Testament calls gentleness. He could have really hurt Jerry, but what was the point? Everyone already knew he was stronger. Malcolm Tolbert spoke about this matter:

> People who are secure in their own persons and in their relationship with God do not lord it over their brothers and sisters. Persons secure in this way identify with others and share their weaknesses and their needs. People marked by lowliness or humility do not think about personal glory but about the welfare of those whom Christ loves.[4]

Thus gentleness and strength go together. If you think about it, you will probably realize that the people who have the most inner strength are some of the most humble and gentle people anywhere. I have a friend who has a black belt in karate, but you would never guess it by looking at him. He does not strut around like a bantam rooster, trying to "make a statement." This friend is aware that he is well capable of defending himself if someone ever tried to hurt him, but he does not show off. Centuries ago, the philosopher Plato realized that gentleness and strength go together. Plato spoke of a watchdog who is bravely hostile to strangers and gently friendly with people he knows and trusts.

The Bible speaks with one voice in its condemnation of aggressive, arrogant pride. This is the opposite of gentleness. Job promises that the Lord will vindicate the justice of the gentle while the arrogant and prideful person will suffer (Job 36:15). The Psalms are replete with such references. Consider these: "The LORD sustains the humble but casts the wicked to the ground" (147:6). "Have mercy on us, O LORD, have mercy on us, for we have endured much contempt. We have endured much ridicule from the proud, much contempt from the arrogant" (123:3-4). Many other references like these exist. "Good and upright is the LORD; therefore he instructs sinners in his ways. He guides the humble in what is right and teaches them his way" (25:8-9).

Many people have memorized Proverbs 3:5-6: "Trust in the LORD with all your heart and lean not on your own understanding; in all your ways acknowledge him, and he will make your paths straight." This counsel helps us to realize that only by acknowledging our weaknesses can we hope to overcome them. As someone opined, "True humility isn't saying that we're dumb and that we can't do anything right, it's *knowing our own weaknesses and struggles, and honestly admitting them.* Standing before the Lord God Almighty, our best strengths are *nothing* compared to His awesome power and wisdom."[5]

Learning Personal Gentleness

Have you ever noticed how different people can be from one another? Some seem calm and serene on the inside and outside; they seem to take life in stride and never get ruffled. For these people, being gentle with others comes easily and naturally. Others are exactly the opposite. They act as if they have just finished their fifteenth cup of coffee, and the caffeine is hitting them. They seem jittery and become upset at the least annoyance. For these folks to display gentleness requires great effort and concentration. The point is, that while some have an easier time with this fruit of the Spirit, most of us must learn how to cultivate it.

Barclay writes that gentleness in the New Testament conveys three main ideas: submission to the will of God; teachableness; and consideration of others.[6] The first two of these are similar. For one to be submissive to the will of God, he must open himself up for God's instruction. As Paul wrote in Ephesians 5:17, "Therefore do not be foolish, but understand what the Lord's will is." Again, some find it easier to do this than others. The plain fact is that some people refuse even to consider anything new or beyond their own current understanding. Dr. Booker T. Washington used to remark that in his educational work, he found three types of ignorance: simple ignorance; don't-know-and-don't-care ignorance; and just plain cussed ignorance!

Learning gentleness is first of all learning about God in a personal relationship. It is opening yourself to learn and experience thoughts, feelings, and will power that you may never have known before. To do this removes you from the narrow-minded precepts of those who feel they have it made and need nothing else. The Lord delivered his judgment on such people through his spokesman Jeremiah: "This is what the LORD says: 'Cursed is the one who trusts in man, who depends on flesh for his strength and whose heart turns away from the LORD' " (17:5). His promise is given through Isaiah: "For this is what the high and lofty One says—he who lives forever, whose name is holy: 'I live in a high and holy place, but also with him who is contrite and lowly in spirit, to revive the spirit of the lowly and to revive the heart of the contrite' " (57:15).

To be gentle is to allow your total self—mind, body, and spirit—to be at the disposal of God. It is to stop rebelling and bucking so that all of your energy can be harnessed for something useful. When you do this, you discover that your trust in God increases because of what He is able to do with and through you. Jeremiah wrote, "This is what the LORD says: 'Let not the wise man boast of his wisdom or the strong man boast of his strength or the rich man boast of his riches, but let him who boasts boast about this: that he understands and knows me, that I am the LORD, who exercises kindness, justice and righteousness on earth, for in these I delight,' declares the LORD" (9:23-24).

Paul understood this, too. He had all the right credentials for bragging about achievements on a worldly basis. But Paul realized that something was more important than personal achievement. That something is a personal relationship with God through Christ. Paul had a physical problem which he called his "thorn in the flesh," and asked God to remove it. This was the answer Paul received: "But he said to me, 'My grace is sufficient for you, for my power is made perfect in weakness.' Therefore I will boast all the more gladly about my weaknesses, so that Christ's power may rest on me. That is why, for Christ's sake, I delight in weaknesses, in insults, in hardships, in persecutions, in difficulties. For when I am weak, then I am strong" (2 Cor. 12:9-10). Paul's gentleness may be seen as weakness by some, but in the eyes of God, it is a "powerful weakness."

As we learn the lesson of gentleness, we should remember to be gentle with ourselves and not to become frustrated when it does not come quickly or easily. Francis de Sales, who lived in France from 1567 until 1622, wrote a book which has become a classic of devotional literature. Its title is *Introduction to the Devout Life*. In this work de Sales realized how easily Christians can become discouraged in their efforts to grow in faith and virtue. Thinking of this, de Sales wrote:

> One of the best exercises of meekness we can perform is that of
> . . . never fretting at our own imperfections; for though reason requires
> that we should be sorry when we commit any fault, yet we must refrain
> from that bitter, gloomy, spiteful, and passionate displeasure for which
> we are greatly to blame, who, being overcome by anger, are angry for
> having been angry and vexed to see ourselves; for by this means we keep
> our hearts perpetually steeped in passion; and though it seems as if the
> second anger destroyed the first, it serves, nevertheless, to open a
> passage for fresh anger on the first occasion that shall present itself.
> Besides, this anger and vexation against ourselves tend to pride, and

flow from no other source than self-love, which is troubled and disquieted to see itself imperfection.

We must be displeased at our faults, but in a peaceable, settled, and firm manner; for, as a judge punishes malefactors much more justly when he is guided in his decisions by reason, and proceeds with the spirit of tranquility than when he acts with violence and passion (because judging in his passion, he does not punish the faults according to their enormity, but according to his passion), so we correct ourselves much better by a calm and steady repentance than by that which is harsh, turbulent, and passionate; for repentance exercised with violence proceeds not according to the quality of our faults but according to our inclinations.[7]

Part of this gentleness is to be shown toward the faults of others, too. Jesus had no kind word for those who could find a speck in their brother's eye but who overlooked the 2 by 4 in their own. On the contrary, He continually preached the gospel of love and peace, which surely includes consideration. You cannot win another person to your viewpoint or your faith by intimidating him. You must attract him with lovingkindness. Paul knew of this and referred to it when writing to his young friend Timothy: "And the Lord's servant must not quarrel; instead, he must be kind to everyone, able to teach, not resentful. Those who oppose him he must gently instruct, in the hope that God will grant them repentance leading them to a knowledge of the truth, and that they will come to their senses and escape from the trap of the devil, who has taken them captive to do his will" (2 Tim. 2:24-5).

I am not sure why it is, but "religion" seems to make some people meaner instead of nicer! When a person feels he has God in his hip pocket, that he has all the answers, and that if you don't see things his way you are obviously wrong and controlled by the devil, there is little hope of such a person winning another through gentle instruction and correction. Some people just will not admit to being wrong, or not knowing something, and will argue and defend their positions even if those positions are ill-informed and absurd.

Dr. Samuel Johnson was an English author who published his *Dictionary of the English Language* in 1755. He was a brilliant man with encyclopedic knowledge and a sharp wit. Yet Johnson would argue with anyone on almost every subject and never back down. One man who knew him well said of him, "The most light and airy dispute was with him a dispute in the arena. He fought on every occasion as if his whole reputation depended upon the victory of the minute, and he fought with all his weapons. If he was foiled in argument, he had recourse to abuse and rudeness." Another commented of him, "There is no arguing with Johnson; for, when his pistol misses fire, he knocks you down with the butt end of it." Still another friend wrote, "There is no disputing with him. He will not hear you, and, having a louder voice than you, must roar you down."[8]

The point of this discussion is to stress the need for intellectual and emotional openness toward God and toward others as we learn to live with gentleness. One reason we have so much trouble with this aspect of spiritual life is: not much in our culture prepares us for it. We are not taught to be gentle but rather to be aggressive and competitive. From the time children are in the first grade, and sometimes earlier, they are put in classes with other youngsters and then taught how to compete for grades and position within the class. Many people learn competition to the extent that they cannot function normally without it. One man I know of was a brilliant student, whizzing through college and graduate school making the top grades. When he finished his Ph.D. he underwent a long period of depression, since there were no more academic mountains to climb. He had reached the top, and had no one else to compete with. He couldn't stand it!

A friend of mine named Mary recently gave me a book entitled *Rhinoceros Success.* Mary signed the book, "To Don, from one Rhino to Another." This book is about how to act like a rhinoceros in the sense of being aggressive, charging, never letting up. The author writes, "The secret of success is, naturally, becoming a rhinoceros. If fact, my wish for you is that you wake up tomorrow morning as a full grown, six-thousand pound rhinoceros!"[9]

These creatures of the jungle charge madly, have thick skin that virtually nothing can penetrate, and in general, scare the blazes out of the competition. I told Mary I appreciated the book, as I always do with the gifts of friends, but I wondered why she thought of me as a rhino. She explained that it is because I never give up, I know what I want to accomplish, and take criticism in stride—all supposedly like a rhino. I mention this book because many people feel as that author does. They are out to make a name, to accomplish greatness, to earn a large paycheck. Always charging and never backing off, many of these people have never learned that even rhinos sometimes enjoy just lying in the mud. Another of my friends is under forty but has vowed to be a millionaire by the time he is fifty. He is driving himself mercilessly and experiencing upsetting conflicts at home and work. To paraphrase an old proverb, all aggression and no gentleness makes Jack a very dull boy.

Sports in America seem to feed what has been called the "killer instinct." Lately this instinct has married Christian teaching, and the offspring has been a sort of theological freak. Boxer Floyd Patterson credited God for helping him knock out Archie Moore to win his heavyweight championship a few years ago. Patterson exclaimed, "I could see his eyes go glassy as he fell back, and I knew if he got up again it wouldn't do him any good. I just hit him and the Lord did the rest."[10] Really? Did the great Lord of the universe care anything about two men trying to knock each other's heads off? Did the One who gave himself in Christ and who went to the cross to prove His love really "do the rest" when Patterson hit his opponent? I doubt it!

We have become so caught up in the sanctification of sports that we seem unable to think straight anymore. I admire the honesty of Doug Plank, formerly a defensive back for the Chicago Bears, who realized that his athletic and religious lives were often in conflict. Plank confided, "As a Christian I learn to love, but when the whistle blows I have to be tough. You're always on a tightrope." At least he realized his dilemma. I have read the New Testament through many times, and I never recall finding one verse that says anything like, "You shall love your neighbor as yourself, except when he is your opponent in an athletic match, at which time you have complete liberty to pulverize him." The late Jim Fixx, whose work was so instrumental in the jogging craze, was impressed by the way runners described their commitment to jogging. They made it sound like a religious conversion experience. One lady told Fixx about her husband's choice to take up running: "Tom used to be a Methodist; now he's a runner."[11]

What, then, are we to think about aggression in sports and Christian faith? Shirl J. Hoffman, in an excellent article entitled "The Sanctification of Sport," offers five suggestions to help us shape our thinking in this matter. First, realize that general Christian ethics cannot fit snugly beside the contemporary sports ethic. Second, realize the sport is an interpersonal experience. Third, the play life of a person tends to be a window through which to view him. How he wins or loses speaks volumes about the rest of him. Fourth, if sport is to be kept as sport, the object of winning must not be deemphasized, but we must not think that God loves only winners. Fifth, the objective of a game is to win, but the reason for participation in sports surpasses a concern for the actual outcome. Participation is more important than winning.

Basketball great "Pistol" Pete Maravich learned fairly late in his life that there is much more to life than winning on the basketball court. When he signed a $1.5 million contract with the Atlanta Hawks, Maravich was at that time the highest-paid rookie in the history of the NBA. He worked hard in his playing, was traded several times, and ended his career in 1980 after playing for the Boston Celtics for one year. Maravich's life was strange, by his own account. He learned karate from a master so he had the ability to kill. He became a Hindu and believed in reincarnation. He then became a believer of UFOism. Still later he tried yoga, survivalism, became a vegetarian, and began drinking heavily. In all of this he was groping for some meaning in his life beyond the basketball court. Then in 1982 he had an encounter with Christ. He confessed, "I woke in the middle of the night in a cold sweat and heard the Lord tell me to be strong in the heart. I was immediately a changed person."[12] He went on, "I found out that there are things more important than basketball. Jesus is the answer. I am now dedicating my life to the Lord and am going out and tell about his great works."

The point of all this discussion is to speak to the issue of gentleness, and to note how this element of spiritual living is often at odds with most of the prevailing philosophies around us. This includes not only sports, but also business. I heard of a man with a sign in his office which read: "If The Meek Inherit the Earth, Then What Will Happen to Us Tigers?"

The New Testament nowhere asks people to roll over and play dead. That is not gentleness—that is laziness. What the New Testament does is to help us retool our thinking and emotions, and to put our inner lives in order. Thus we can live in this grace-filled manner which is called gentleness. Whether or not we make giant impacts on the world is hardly the point. Charles Kingsley penned these words, "We are surely not sent into the world to get credit and reputations, but to speak such words as are given us to do; not heeding much, nor expecting to know whether they have effected anything or nothing. Therefore friends, be of good courage."[13]

Saint Teresa lived from 1515 until 1582. She headed up a group of nuns and wrote spiritual books and tracts to help them live gentle lives in Christ. In one of her works Teresa offered the following advice to the self-important:

> It is very important for us to realize that God does not lead us all by the same road. . . . Remember that there must be someone to cook the meals and count yourselves happy in being able to serve like Martha. Reflect that true humility consists to a great extent in being ready for what the Lord desires to do with you.
>
> Remember that the Lord walks among the pots and pans and that He will help you in the inward tasks and in the outward too.[14]

The world seems full of "important" people who push and shove and scramble for the top. Christ emerges from the pages of the New Testament as our eternal contemporary who urges us to do our best but never to seek the places of honor. He bids us come and die with Him, and in so doing, we will find authentic life. His gentleness inspires us to imitate Him. Gentleness truly is the most powerful of weaknesses.

9

Stifle Yourself—
Self-Control

*If you would learn self-mastery, begin by yielding yourself to the
One Great Master.—Johann Friedrich Lobstein*

The old television program, *All in the Family,* featured Archie and
Edith Bunker as the main characters. Archie was an opinionated,
loud, and obnoxious bigot. Edith was a rather quiet, gentle soul who
usually gave in to her husband's overbearing demands. One of the
most obnoxious things Archie would say to Edith was "Edit', stifle
yourself!" This became his stock reply when she would say what
Archie didn't want to hear.

The word *stifle* itself has a nerve-jarring sound to it. It comes from
the old French *estouffer* which means to smother or choke. One
dictionary defines it as: "To kill by preventing respiration; smother or
suffocate." What does all this have to do with the fruit of the Spirit?
Some people seem to feel that the last in the list—self-control—is
similar to Archie's demand of Edith. Some people have an image of
God sitting on a throne in heaven to human beings, "Hey, you down
there. Stifle yourself!" However, when Paul listed self-control among
the fruit of the Spirit, he had no such idea in mind. His concept was
not harsh and strident but was given for the well-being of those who
learn to control themselves.

Understanding Self-Control

In centuries gone by the church sometimes thought of self-control
in terms of severe discipline. Four general uses for this term were
given by the ancient church.[1] Discipline sometimes meant a way of
life which was prescribed by the church and embodied in various rules
and regulations. Second, discipline referred to forms of asceticism and
mortification, such as self-beatings and living in monasteries. Third,

it came to refer to a scourge, a whip of knotted cords used to enforce discipline. Last, it was a way of life prescribed by the church and enforced on practitioners. For example, when the Reformation leader John Calvin lived in Geneva he used his position to enforce severe discipline on the inhabitants of that city. It did not work for long, and Calvin was forced to flee Geneva.

The point of this is: what Paul meant by "self-control" was misunderstood by some of our spiritual ancestors. Think of all of the other elements of the fruit of the Spirit. Are any of them harsh or ugly? Love, joy, peace, patience, kindness, goodness, faithfulness, gentleness —these are all positive and healthy values. So with self-control, too. It refers to a simple fact of life. You and I cannot have everything, do everything, or experience everything. We are limited in our time, our finances, and our ability to respond to various experiences. To be self-controlled is to acknowledge that not everything is good for you, and therefore it is to choose wisely and carefully among life's smorgasbord. Paul wrote to Timothy: "For God did not give us a spirit of timidity, but a spirit of power, of love and of self-discipline" (2 Tim. 1:7). Paul referred here to a reasoned, well-ordered life. Discipline, self-discipline, and self-control are all similar concepts in the New Testament. None refers to a life which is lived in isolation from Christ, but they all put the responsibility for how we live squarely on our shoulders.

Here is one of the great paradoxes of our faith. On the one hand we live in the Spirit. We are under His influence and guidance. As Paul wrote in Galatians 2:20, "I have been crucified with Christ and I no longer live, but Christ lives in me. The life I live in the body, I live by faith in the Son of God, who loved me and gave himself for me." On the other hand, *we* actually live. We are not dead nor are we zombies. Ultimately we have to take responsibility for our lives. We cannot blame God for our failures. As James reminded us, "When tempted, no one should say, 'God is tempting me.' For God cannot be tempted by evil, nor does he tempt anyone; but each one is tempted when, by his own evil desire, he is dragged away and enticed" (1:13-14). To mature in faith is to trust God and also to live the best we can, but always to be responsible for our actions.

Fred Craddock once said that there is no way to modulate the human voice to make a whine acceptable to God. I think what he means is that we waste our time and God's when we try to evade responsible for what we are and what we do. It is far better to affirm with Paul, "By God's grace, I am what I am" (1 Cor. 15:10). In my opinion, people who refuse to take responsibility for themselves, who try to blame God for their mistakes and problems, are just "spiritual brats."

To be self-controlled does not mean, of course, that I do whatever I want to without a thought of God or the welfare of others. This part of the fruit of the Spirit is not a license to be irresponsible. Too many times people have sought to be completely self-controlled in the sense of being self-centered. This if *far* from what Paul had in mind. William Ernest Henley, in his poem "Invictus," wrote: "I am the master of my fate, I am the captain of my soul."

Really? I think no man can be master of himself until he acknowledges Christ as his ultimate Master. Morgan Phelps Noyes thought about the sentiment expressed in Henley's poem and wrote, "No man is the master of his fate so long as he lives in a universe which he did not create, and no man is the captain of his soul so long as there are within him dark forces which need to be redeemed."[2] Noyes was right on target. You and I are not totally free. We are influenced by impulses and forces both within and outside of ourselves. We need to be aware of and sensitive to these influences and not let them control our lives.

Too many people seem to wander around aimlessly, without any sense of inner purpose or goals. They drift from one fad to the next, from one lover to the next, from one job to the next, without really knowing what they want or how to achieve it. The fruit of the Spirit, and especially self-control, takes life out of the realm of chance or the impulse of the moment. It puts life on the level of the long-range view. This is actually a theological issue. If life has no ultimate meaning and if God does not exist, then I am perfectly free simply to follow every impulse or desire I might have. As Paul put it when quoting pagan philosophy, "Let us eat and drink, for tomorrow we die" (1 Cor. 15:33). I can eat anything and everything because health would be irrelevant. I could become sexually involved with as many women as I might wish because faithfulness to my wife would have no meaning. I would not be concerned with working hard and doing my best because such standards would be absurd.

All of this would be true *if* God does not exist and *if* life has no meaning. But I believe that God lives and that life somehow makes sense. Therefore, I am enabled to take a long-range view of life. I do not eat anything and everything because all is not good for me, and I do not want to get overweight and develop high blood pressure. I do not allow my normal and natural sexual desires to get out of hand because I value my exclusive relationship with my wife much more than the fleeting pleasures of promiscuity. I try to work hard and do my best because I feel that what I do is important to others, as well as to myself.

Self-control, then, is a wholistic view of looking at life. It begins with a personal relationship with God through faith in Christ. It moves to the level of a disciplined mind. I am not referring primarily to trying to suppress certain thoughts. What I have in mind is the fact that the human mind does not operate well in neutral. It always is thinking, evaluating, planning, hoping. The key to disciplining the mind is not simply to remove certain thoughts but rather to replace them with better thoughts. The writer, John Erskine, said, "Though we sometimes speak of a primrose path, we all know that a bad life is just as difficult, just as full of work, obstacles and hardships, as a good one. The only choice is the kind of life one would care to spend one's efforts on."[3] He is right, of course. Since a bad life is just as difficult—and I really think *more* difficult—why not spend our time and energy on something of worth and value?

This means we must learn to break out of the web of habits. Psychologist Denis Waitley speaks of this:

> Habits start out as off-hand remarks, magazine advertisements, friendly hints, experiments—like flimsy cobwebs with little substance. They grow with practice, layer upon layer—thought upon thought—fused with imagination and emotion until they become like steel cables

—unbreakable. Habits are attitudes which grow from cobwebs into cables that control your everyday life.

Self-discipline alone can make or break a habit. Self-discipline alone can effect a permanent change in your self-image and in you. Self-discipline achieves goals.

Many people define self-discipline as "doing without." A better definition for discipline is "doing within." Self-discipline is mental practice —the commitment to memory of those thoughts and emotions that will override current information stored in the subconscious memory bank.[4]

Waitley is moving in the right direction. Self-control is not just stopping myself from doing something, but more positively, helping myself to do something better. It begins with a disciplined imagination that allows me to "see" something better and therefore to reach out for it. The Christian need not fear the imagination, because like every other aspect of human life, it has enormous power for moral good, as well as for evil. The fact is that we all have an imagination whether or not we do anything with it or not. Why not put it to disciplined use in service for Christ?

One of the most influential Christian leaders during the first third of this century was S. Parkes Cadman. He wrote two books on the subject of imagination and its relationship to spiritual life. In one of these books Cadman noted:

Man as the self-conscious animal is the saddest spectacle extant; whereas man as the convinced son of God is the noblest. Why reflect hypochondria, diseased notions, or loathsome dreams when the strength and beauty of an ordered imagination, submissive to the things of the spirit, is at our command? The approval of temperance, truthfulness and courage, and the condemnation of the reverse qualities are instinctive and immediate to the imagination. "To the pure all things are pure," and these are vouchsafed them by their vision of God.[5]

How easy it is to allow ourselves to drift along rather than allowing God to take command of our lives! Waitley said, "I didn't realize until I was thirty-five that I'm behind the wheel in my life. I thought it was the government, inflation and my heritage. I used to think that as a

Gemini, I was destined to be creative, but non-specific."[6] Think about it. Who, or what, controls your life? Do you read the horoscope each morning to see what you can or cannot do that day? Do you ask permission from your spouse, your children, or your parents before you do anything? Do you brood regularly on how "they"—whomever "they" might be—are in your way or block your happiness or interfere with your life? One means of gaining some sense of self-control is to specify exactly and specifically what and who seems to be blocking your potential for creative living. Then the next step would be to brainstorm ways of going around or through that blockage. This doesn't mean that you suddenly begin ignoring your family or telling your employer to jump in the lake. What I mean is that you try to gain an objective perspective on your life. None of us can live in absolute and total control of our lives. We are born to parents whom we did not choose, live lives that are influenced by thousands of outside factors, and die at times which we have little to do with. Every birth certificate comes with an expiration date! The key is not to let others steal your life!

Self-control also has to do with our emotional lives. If our emotions are severely damaged we can find help through trained medical and mental-health professionals. One positive thing which has happened in recent years is that the stigma of mental problems has begun to fade. People who seek help for emotional and mental problems are no longer labeled as "crazy" or "nuts." The human mind is a delicate and finely-tuned organ, and it can become imbalanced fairly easily. I have seen troubled people virtually remade through the help of caring mental-health specialists. If your emotional or intellectual life seems beyond your self-control, please realize that there is no shame in seeking help.

People sometimes yell things like, "He makes me so mad!" and then they fly off into a rage of uncontrolled emotional outburst. I sometimes think of this as an emotional "meltdown." Self-control, as part of the fruit of the Spirit of God, helps us avoid the outbursts. Look at a biblical example. In the Old Testament, Gideon gathered the various tribes of Israel and went into battle. But the tribe of the Ephraimites somehow were left out, and after the battle they responded: "Now the Ephraimites asked Gideon, 'Why have you treated us like this? Why didn't you call us when you went to fight Midian?' And they criticized him sharply" (Judg. 8:1). Gideon could have exploded and answered: "You idiots! Don't you know how busy I was? Don't you realize how important swift action was? You termites! You have no right to criticize me!" But look at what he actually said: " 'What have I accomplished compared to you? Aren't the gleanings of Ephraim's grapes better than the full grape harvest of Abiezer? God gave Oreb and Zeeb, the Midianite leaders, into your hands. What was I able to do compared to you?' At this, their resentment against him subsided" (Judg. 8:2-3). His self-control accomplished all he wanted, including easing the anger of his fellow countrymen and also maintaining his leadership. Phillips Elliott commented on Gideon's self-control in this situation and then make an application to Christian faith:

> If one wants to find the clearest test of greatness, can he do better than observing a man's humility? The proud man is the little man. The humble man is the big man. Wherever true humility resides, even though without secular acclaim, the marks of greatness can be seen. It is uniquely the mark of the Christian.[7]

To be a Christian does not mean that we are emotionless or listless. Far from it! It means instead that all of the emotional and mental energy we possess is channeled into constructive activities and purposes. Horse trainers are aware that almost nothing can be done with a wild horse. It may possess tremendous strength, but that strength means little until the horse is broken and all that energy is focused in a specific direction. A horse which has been broken is no less powerful than an unbroken one. The difference lies in the fact that its power and energy are pulled together and focused into a set task such as being a mount.

This is true of persons, too. The difference between an athlete and a nonathlete may not be in physical strength. The fellow who drinks a case of beer each day and does nothing more strenuous than watching football on TV may be fully strong as the man who earns his living on the gridiron. The difference is that the athlete has the self-discipline and self-control to keep himself in top shape and to focus his strength in one direction. I mentioned in the previous chapter the difference between a river and a swamp; that difference is applicable here, too. The TV watcher is like the swamp, and the disciplined athlete is like the river.

Proverbs 16:32 makes an astounding affirmation: "Better a patient man than a warrior, a man who controls his temper than one who takes a city." Think of that. Keeping control over your temper is more pivotal, and perhaps harder, than being a victor in battle. Other proverbs support this claim. Proverbs 14:29 says, "A patient man has great understanding, but a quick-tempered man displays folly." Proverbs 19:11 notes, "A man's wisdom gives him patience; it is to his glory to overlook an offense," and 29:11 advises, "A fool gives vent to his anger, but a wise man keeps himself under control." Rolland Schloerb was right on target when he commented on these Proverbs this way:

> In fact, self-control might be considered the highest kind of power. A man may find himself in a position where he can exercise power over other people, but if he has not learned how to control himself, his power may bring disaster. "He who rules his spirit" is better "than he who takes a city." Having taken the city, the person without self-restraint may ruin it by a foolish outburst of temper. He can hardly be trusted to rule over others because he has not learned how to rule himself.
>
> The wise person can direct his/her feelings of indignation into constructive channels. The person who has fits of temper is not necessarily more indignant than another person. The other person may control twice as much feeling, but direct it like the explosions in the cylinders of a gasoline motor.[8]

Finding the Will Power

The biblical concept of self-control is not a "bootstrap" philosophy in which one simply make up his mind to be better and thereby solve all his problems. The Bible is the most realistic book ever written. None of its writers expected human perfection in this life. While some popular psychology seems to suggest that people can will their problems away, most psychologists are realistic enough to comprehend the depths of our human dilemma. Carl G. Jung, the well-known pioneer in psychological studies, wrote, "We are unable, for example, to suppress many of our emotions; we cannot change a bad mood into a good mood, and we cannot command our dreams to come or go. We only believe that we are masters in our own house because we like to flatter ourselves."9

In order to develop self-control we have to find the will power. We need to desire this aspect of spiritual living so much that we are willing to work, sweat, and sacrifice to make progress—all under the indwelling power of God. One approach is to consider the lives of those who have exercised self-control, then to visualize yourself responding similarly. Look, for example, at Booker T. Washington as recounted in his autobiography, *Up from Slavery*. Washington was born a slave but was freed after the Civil War. He wrote of his hunger for an education and how he was willing to do whatever it took to get it. This remarkable man remembered his days on the plantation and recalled that the system of slavery bred a spirit of laziness and lack of discipline in many of the slave owners' families.

The slave system on our place, in a large measure, took the spirit of self-reliance and self-help out of the white people. My old master had many boys and girls, but not one, so far as I know, ever mastered a single trade or special line of productive industry. The girls were not taught to cook, sew, or to take care of the house. All this was left to the slaves. The slaves, of course, had little personal interest in the life of the plantation, and their ignorance prevented them from learning how to do things in the most improved and thorough manner. As a result of the system, fences were out of repair, gates were hanging half off the hinges, doors creaked, window-panes were out, plastering had fallen but was not replaced, weeds grew in the yard. As a rule, there was food for whites and blacks, but inside the house, and on the dining-room table, there was wanting that delicacy and refinement of touch and finish which can make a home the most convenient, comfortable, and attractive place in the world. Withal there was a waste of food and other materials which was sad. When freedom came, the slaves were almost as well fitted to begin life anew as the master, except in the matter of book-learning and ownership of property. The slave owner and his sons had mastered no special industry. They unconsciously had imbibed the feeling that manual labour was not the proper thing for them. On the other hand, the slaves, in many cases, had mastered some handicraft, and none were ashamed, and few unwilling, to labour.[10]

The lesson here is that we cannot depend on others to do everything for us. We must take care of ourselves. When I consider Washington's plight and what he endured, I am inspired to do my own best. Part of self-control is the determination to do what I can for myself.

Consider the life of Glenn Cunningham. One cold February morning in 1916, Glenn, then seven, and his older brother Floyd entered their school room to make a fire in the potbellied stove. Floyd poured what he thought was kerosene on what seemed to be cold wood. Later they learned a community club had met in the school the night before and used the stove. Also, someone had put gasoline in the kerosene can. When Floyd poured it on the wood, it exploded and burned him and Glenn badly.

The doctor came, examined both boys, and told the family that if infection set in he would have to amputate Glenn's legs. He also admitted there was not much he could do for Floyd. The two boys lay in their beds, talked and sang hymns, but seldom moved. One the ninth morning after the accident, Floyd died. Three months later Glenn still could not move his legs or bend his knees, but his mother massaged his scarred limbs every day.

Glenn's father was a good runner, and they would talk about running. This gave Glenn a goal to focus his hopes on; he made up his mind that he *would* walk again—and not only that, he would run. After six months passed, Glenn's father put a big chair in the boy's room that became a brace and exercise station. Each day he would pull himself out of bed, hold on to the sides of that chair, and stretch and bend. On the day before Christmas, Glenn told his mother that he had a Christmas present for her, but she would have to stand by the door and close her eyes. She did so, and Glenn took a few faltering steps toward her. She reached out for him as they both slumped to the floor together.

By the next spring his family had moved to another community, and Glenn had a two-mile walk to and from school. This helped loosen his legs, but he still could not run without pain. Nevertheless, he kept trying. By the time he was twelve he entered the school's track meet. All of the other boys were high school students, but Glenn wanted to compete with them anyway. He not only kept up with them but also passed them and won that race!

It was not his last race to win. Glenn Cunningham went on to win an Olympic medal and to set world records for the 800-meter race and the mile. He and his wife Ruth established the Cunningham Youth Ranch in Cedar Point, Kansas, where for thirty years they helped more than nine-thousand troubled youths.[11]

The message in all of this? Never give up! Never quit! Never take no for an answer! Self-control means allowing God to master you to the point of not allowing disappointments, and even tragedies, to deter you from your ultimate goals and dreams. God's power is available to His children. As Paul exulted, "I can do everything through him who gives me strength" (Phil. 4:13).

Dealing with Everything in Life

"The fruit of the Spirit is . . . self-control." This is such an amazing statement. God wants for His children to live above the level of physical cravings; He wants them to live intentionally—that is, to formulate principles, guidelines, and goals for life, and then to follow them. All else leads to trouble.

Proverbs 5:20-23 is a father's advice to his son, urging him to exercise self-control about women. The father says, "Why be captivated, my son, by an adulteress? Why embrace the bosom of another man's wife? For a man's ways are in full view of the LORD, and he examines all his paths. The evil deeds of a wicked man ensnare him; the cords of his sin hold him fast. *He will die for lack of discipline,* led astray by his own great folly" (Italics added). By the same token, women should avoid the wiles of a male adulterer.

A friend of mine once told me about his early life. He had to get married because his girl friend was pregnant. Their marriage was shaky from the start and ended in divorce. This friend later married again, and told me something shortly before his wedding I will never forget: "You know, Don, it's taken me a long time to learn, but I've finally decided to start thinking with my mind instead of with my sex organs!" He had finally received the grace gift of self-control in his life.

This fruit of the Spirit allows you to cultivate talents and insights that are uniquely yours, and then to use those for the cause of Christ. Each of us is as individual as our fingerprints. You can do things no one else can do in exactly the same fashion. I mentioned earlier that self-control is not primarily negative in Archie Bunker's sense— "Stifle yourself!" Instead, this quality of discipline is positive because it allows us to focus our abilities instead of dissipate them. Ernest T. Campbell presented a prayer thanking God for the unique gifts which various people have brought to the church. I close this chapter with this prayer, and add to it my own "Amen" because Campbell is right on target. May God grant us the courage to be self-controlled for His sake as well as our own.

> We bless Thee for Thy church,
>   one in the Holy Spirit
>   yet richly varied in its several parts.
> We remember in a single breath of gratitude:
>   The disciplined thought of Aquinas;
>   The carefree simplicity of St. Francis;
>   The raging discontent of Luther;
>   The expository gifts of Calvin;
>   The prayer life of St. Theresa;
>   The enthusiasm of the Wesleys;
>   The pregnant silence of George Fox;
>   The conscience of Leo Tolstoy;
>   The stirring utterances and courageous
>   actions of Martin Luther King, Jr.;
>   The poems of Marianne Moore;
>   The plays of T. S. Eliot;
>   The social vision of Camile Torres.
> Add to Thy church in every place, O God,
>   such as will love Thee with all their powers,

For we yearn to see embodied
    the kind of faith that can move mountains
    and set Thy people free.
Through Jesus Christ Our Lord, Amen.[12]

10
Living in the Spirit, Walking in the Spirit: Epilogue

Thus we have examined Galatians 5:22, the fruit of the Spirit. Each element of the Spirit as listed in that verse is one aspect of a well-rounded and balanced Christian life. Who could imagine, for example, such a life devoid of love or peace or patience? These are the basics of Christian living.

In the next two verses, Paul continued to write about living in the Spirit: "Those who belong to Christ Jesus have crucified the sinful nature with its passions and desires. Since we live by the Spirit, let us keep in step with the Spirit." This is both a statement of theological truth and a request. What did Paul mean? In this last section, I want to look into Paul's meaning.

To "walk" in the Spirit means to live in, trust in, and act on what you believe as the truth of God. It means continually to choose the path of spiritual life. It is to interweave your life with the life of God to the extent that you become sensitive to His presence. Malcolm Tolbert notes, "The word *walk* encompasses attitudes, relationships, actions, goals—in short, all the way in which a person expresses his or her being."[1] He also states, "*Walk* . . . stands for conduct. The term embraces attitudes, acts, and relationships. The specific idea is related to the believer's life in the body of Christ."[2] To walk in the Spirit, then, is to develop an attitude and life-style which is sensitive to and quickened by the Spirit.

Some people try to live by the Law. The trouble with that is the Law, as exemplified by an encoded tradition, is dead. Paul declared in Romans 2:13-15 that such Law has no internal power over us. Others try to live by the Ten Commandments. This is helpful but

119

inadequate by itself. Paul noted in 2 Corinthians 3:12-13 that the power of the Ten Commandments alone, as delivered by Moses, has faded like the shine on Moses' face. The alternative to trying to live up to some external authority or guideline is to have an *internal* Guide, the Spirit.

To walk in the Spirit is to experience the freedom He gives. This is both freedom *from* and freedom *for*. It is freedom from the dominance of sin. It is also freedom for ethical and righteous living.

> Freedom in Christ is not freedom to do what I like, but freedom to be what I am meant to be. It is freedom from all the chains which hold me back from being my true self. It is freedom from all imposed limitations and external pressures. It is to share in Christ's freedom to do God's will, and then to help others find a similar freedom.[3]

The slogan, "Be all that you can be," applies not only to the United States Army, but also to the Christian army!

Someone is always wanting to control your life. You might as well come to grips with this fact. Even in the church I find people who want to control me and manipulate me, so I try be sensitive not to do that to others. You see, the church is Christ's and not mine or yours. To live in the Spirit means that I surrender my life to no one except Christ. I cannot surrender my life to my spouse, to my career, to my children, to my friends, or any other *person*. This doesn't mean that I refuse to listen to them or try to shut them out emotionally. Far from it. I need my family and my friends. What I am referring to is that I have only one life and that many forces are pulling at it. Some of those forces are good and some are not good. So I must be careful what or who I allow to influence me. This choosing is part of what living in the Spirit implies.

To walk in the Spirit is also to experience liberation which allows us to love others. This is absolutely basic. To love others is to invest ourselves in them, to allow them space and time for growth and change, even if that means they grow away from us.

To walk in the Spirit is to remember that any of our perspectives are limited. We must, then, keep a proper humility about us. None of us knows it all and has life put together in a nice bundle. Even the apostle Paul realized his limitations. When the people in Corinth asked him about certain matters related to marriage, Paul responded with a word which he called his own (See 2 Cor. 7:25 and 40). He could have spoken as if his opinion were the final authority. Instead, he told the Corinthians that his word on their question was his opinion and his personal judgment. He spoke with a sense of certainty but not unbending dogmatism. Let him who has ears hear!

An old church leader used to comment, "It's not how high you jump that counts, but how straight you walk when you come back down." There is a world of wisdom in this folksy proverb. Most of us can hit the stratosphere once in a while. It is our terrestrial ramblings that give us the trouble. This is why we need to concentrate on the basics of Christian living. My wedding ring has three words and three symbols on the outside: the word "Faith" with a cross; "Hope" with an anchor; and "Love" with a heart. These words and symbols help me remember who I am and what my commitments are. This is also true with the basics of the Spirit.

Godspeed to you as you allow the Lord to cultivate the fruit of the Spirit in your life. My hope and prayer is that these aspects of spiritual life become living realities for you.

Notes

Preface

1. John Baillie, quoted in *Journey for a Soul* by George Appleton (Glasgow: William Collins & Co., 1974), p. 222.

Chapter 1

1. Francis de Sales, *Introduction to the Devout Life,* in *Living Selections from the Great Devotional Classics* (Nashville: The Upper Room, 1962), p. 14.

2. Orlo Strunk, Jr., *The Secret Self* (Nashville: Abingdon Press, 1976), p. 16. Used by permission of the journal in which it originally appeared, *Pilgrimage,* 427 Lakeshore Drive, Atlanta, GA 30307.

3. Margery Williams, *The Velveteen Rabbit* (Philadelphia: Running Press, 1981), pp. 14-15. Used by permission of the publisher.

Chapter 2

1. William Morrice, *Joy in the New Testament* (Grand Rapids, MI: Eerdmans Publishing Co., 1984).

2. John Wesley, *Selections from the Journal of John Wesley,* arranged and edited by Paul Lambourne Higgins. *Living Selections from the Great Devotional Classics* (Nashville: The Upper Room, 1967), p. 26.

3. Christiaan N. Barnard, "In Celebration of Being Alive," *Reader's Digest,* April 1980, p. 16. Used by permission of the author.

4. Henri J. M. Nouwen, *The Wounded Healer* (Garden City, NY: Image Books, 1979), p. 84. Used by permission.

5. William Blake, quoted in *A Treasury of the Kingdom,* compiled by E. A. Blackburn and others (New York: Oxford University Press, 1954), p. 132.

6. Ibid., p. 127.

7. Associated Press story from Thursday, January 30, 1986.

8. L. D. Johnson, *Moments of Reflection* (Nashville: Broadman Press, 1980), p. 47.

9. Quoted in *Speaker's Illustrations for Special Days,* edited by Charles L. Wallis (New York: Abingdon Press, 1956), p. 164.

Chapter 3

1. This story was written by James O'Byrne in (New Orleans) *The Times-Picayune/ The States Item,* September 17, 1985, pp. A-17-18.

2. Editorial by Lynn P. Clayton, *Baptist Message,* October 31, 1985, p. 4.

3. P. L. Garlick, *Pioneers of the Kingdom,* excerpted in *A Treasury of the Kingdom,* compiled by E. A. Blackburn (New York: Oxford University Press, 1954), pp. 120-212.

4. These statistics come from a study published by World Priorities, an economic research group. The report was summarized by the Associated Press, November 8, 1985.

5. These statistics come from a report on "Entertainment This Week," aired on August 25, 1985.

6. Kenneth S. Kantzer, editorial in *Christianity Today,* December 13, 1985, p. 18.

7. From a story by William J. Shaw, "From Shells into Bells," *The Student,* December, 1985, p. 44.

Chapter 4

1. John Testrake, "Flight 847—My Story," in *Guideposts,* May 1986, p. 7.

2. J. I. Packer, "A Bad Trip," in *Christianity Today,* March 16, 1986, p. 12.

3. William Barclay, *Flesh and Spirit: An Examination of Galatians 5:19-23* (Grand Rapids, MI: Baker Book House, 1976 [1962]), p. 96.

4. This assessment of Mozart in the film is given by Cornelius Plantinga, Jr., in "How Odd of God," in *Christianity Today,* April 19, 1985, p. 32.

5. Ibid.

6. Chrysostom, quoted in *A Treasury of the Kingdom*, compiled by E. A. Blackburn (New York: Oxford University Press, 1954), pp. 144-145.

7. Grant quoted in an essay, "Who Is Buried in Grant's Tomb?" by Lance Morrow in *Time,* September 16, 1985, p. 92.

8. Don Honig, quoted in an article, "The Man Pete Rose Chased—and Caught," by Furman Bisher in *Sky,* November 1985, p. 124.

9. This ancient story I found in *The Talmud,* a Jewish commentary, and is retold several places.

Chapter 5

1. Oscar Wilde, quoted in *Creative Brooding* by Robert Raines, (New York: Collier Books, 1966), p. 86.

2. Gerald Kennedy, *Second Reader's Notebook* (New York: Harper & Brothers, 1954, n.p.n.

3. From *How Can I Help? Stories and Reflections on Service* by Ram Dass and Paul Gorman (New York: Alfred A. Knopf, 1985), p. 54.

4. See a splendid article on this, "A Legacy of Rainbows" by Aletha Jane Lindstrom

in "Focus on the Family," April 1986, pp. 12-13; also in *Reader's Digest,* December 1984.

Chapter 6

1. Cited in *The Friendship Factor* by Alan Loy McGinnis (Minneapolis, MN: Augsburg Publishing House, 1979), p. 15.

2. The word which is translated "goodness" in Galatians 5:22 is *agatosuna* in Greek. It means "generosity" as well as "goodness." *A Greek-English Lexicon of the New Testament and Other Early Christian Literature,* translated and edited by W. F. Arndt and F. W. Gingrich (Chicago: University of Chicago Press, 1957, Fourth Edition), p. 3.

3. Spencer Marsh, *God, Man, and Archie Bunker* (New York: Bantam Books, 1975), pp. 14-16.

4. Quoted in *The Interpreter's Bible* (New York: Abingdon Press, 1954), Volume 11, p. 94.

5. Ibid., p. 13.

6. Sheldon Kopp, *If You Meet the Buddha on the Road, Kill Him!* (New York: Bantam Books, 1976 [1972]), p. 193.

7. The Church Training module, "Discovering Your Spiritual Gifts," published by The Sunday School Board of the Southern Baptist Convention, is helpful here. For further information on knowing and doing the will of God, see these books: *The Will of God* by Morris Ashcraft (Nashville: Broadman Press, 1979) and *Knowing and Doing the Will of God* by Jerry Glisson (Nashville: Broadman Press, 1986).

8. Herman Melville, quoted in *The Interpreter's Bible,* Volume 11 (New York: Abingdon Press, 1955), p. 94.

9. See Arthur Miller's *The Crucible.*

10. This poll was reported in *USA WEEKEND,* February 14-16, 1986, p. 22. Of those polled, 2.1 percent reported, "Don't know or have no answer."

11. Paul Tournier, *Creative Suffering,* translated by Edwin Hudson (San Francisco: Harper & Row, 1982), pp. 94-95.

Chapter 7

1. William Barclay, *Flesh and Spirit* (Grand Rapids, MI: Baker Book House, 1976 [1962]), pp. 107-108.

2. Ibid., p..111.

3. This anonymous prayer is from an article by Anita Deyneka, "God in the Gulag," in *Christianity Today,* August 9, 1985, p. 31.

4. Flannery O'Connor, in *The Habit of Being,* quoted by Paul W. Nisly, in "Faith Is Not an Electric Blanket," in *Christianity Today,* May 17, 1985, p. 24.

5. Doug McCray, "Death Watch: A Journal by Doug McCrary," in *The Plough,* May/June 1986, p. 17. This interview originally appeared in the book, *Slow Coming Dark* by Doug Magee (New York: Pilgrim Press, 1980).

6. If you are troubled by anger at another person, you might turn to Alan Loy McGinnis' helpful book, *The Friendship Factor,* Chapter 13.

7. Lewis B. Smedes, "Controlling the Unpredictable: The Power of Promising," in *Christianity Today,* January 21, 1983, pp. 16-19.

8. Maltbie D. Babcock, in *Treasury of Courage and Confidence* edited by Norman Vincent Peale. Abridged Version (Anderson, IN: Warner Press, 1974), p. 75.

9. Royalites from books are not usually large. A study of 2,239 authors was made by Columbia University. The study found that the average writer earned only $4,774 per year, a poverty scale. See the book I wrote with Len Goss, *Writing Religiously: A Guide to Writing Nonfiction Religious Books* (Milford, MI: Mott Media, 1984), chapter 6.

Chapter 8

1. William Barclay, *Flesh and Spirit* (Grand Rapids: Baker Book House, 1976 [1962]), p. 121.

2. Phil Barnhart, *Seasonings for Sermons* (Lima, OH: C. S. S. Publishing Co., 1980), p. 77.

3. Sheldon Vanauken, *A Severe Mercy* (New York: Bantam Books, 1979 (1977)), p. 88.

4. Malcolm O. Tolbert, *Ephesians: God's New People* (Nashville: Convention Press, 1979), p. 89.

5. Martin Bennett, "Walking in Weakness the Path of the Mighty" in *The Last Days* magazine, Vol. 9, No 1, 1986, p. 11.

6. William Barclay, *Letters to Galatians and Ephesians, Daily Study Bible* (Edinburgh: The Saint Andrew's Press, 1954), p. 56-57.

7. Francis de Sales, *Selections from Introduction to the Devout Life,* arranged and edited by Thomas S. Kepler. *Living Selections from the Great Devotional Classics* (Nashville: The Upper Room, 1962), pp. 23-24.

8. These recollections of Johnson are recounted in Barclay, *Flesh and Spirit,* p. 113.

9. Scott Alexander, *Rhinoceros Success* (Laguna Hills, CA: The Rhino's Press, 1980), p. 11.

10. Floyd Patterson, quoted in an article by Shirl J. Hoffman, "The Sanctification of Sport: Can the Mind of Christ Coexist with the Killer Instinct?" in *Christianity Today,* April 4, 1986, p. 18.

11. Ibid., p. 20.

12. Interview with Pete Maravich in *The Bogalusa* (LA) *Daily News,* May 19, 1986, p. 10.

13. Charles Kingsley, quoted in *The Interpreter's Bible,* Volume IV. (New York: Abingdon Press, 1954), p. 896.

14. St. Teresa, from *The Way of Perfection and the Foundations,* in *A Treasury of the Kingdom,* edited by E. A. Blackburn (New York: Oxford University Press, 1954), p. 197.

Chapter 9

1. *The Westminster Dictionary of Theology,* s. v. "Discipline."